LIVING RHYTHMS

MCGILL-QUEEN'S NATIVE AND NORTHERN SERIES
BRUCE G. TRIGGER, EDITOR

Living Rhythms

Lessons in Aboriginal Economic Resilience and Vision

WANDA WUTTUNEE

McGill-Queen's University Press
Montreal & Kingston • London • Ithaca

© McGill-Queen's University Press 2004
isbn 0-7735-2753-2 (cloth)
isbn 0-7735-2754-0 (paper)

Legal deposit third quarter 2004
Bibliothèque nationale du Québec

Printed in Canada on acid-free paper that is 100% ancient forest free
(100% post-consumer recycled), processed chlorine free.

This book has been published with the help of a grant from the Canadian
Federation for the Humanities and Social Sciences, through the Aid to
Scholarly Publications Programme, using funds provided by the Social Sci-
ences and Humanities Research Council of Canada.

McGill-Queen's University Press acknowledges the financial support of the
Canada Council for the Arts for our publishing program. It also acknowl-
edges the financial support of the Government of Canada through the Book
Publishing Industry Development (BPIDP) for its publishing activities.

National Library of Canada Cataloguing in Publication

Wuttunee, Wanda A. (Wanda Ann), 1956–
Living rhythms: lessons in aboriginal economic resilience
and vision / Wanda Wuttunee.

Includes bibliographical references and index.
ISBN 0-7735-2753-2 (cloth)
ISBN 0-7735-2754-0 (paper)

1. Indians of North America – Canada – Economic conditions.
2. Community development – Canada. I. Title.

E.78.C2W882 2004   330.089'97071   C2004-902114-1

This book was typeset by Dynagram Inc. in 10/13 Sabon.

STAR CHILDREN

The sound is there – in your heart
In your head
It is in the living breath
that is shared with brothers and sisters.

Celebration, gratitude for gifts
so sweet notes of hope echo softly
and slip twinkling, sparkling in the
glitter bright sunlight to dance, to chant.

Deep into the Earth Mother's bosom
Spread your arms out and farther than that
To Grandmother Moon and Grandfather Sun
To the star children and beyond.

Voices meet, mingle, entwine into one.
Pain, fear, greed, sadness are gently
accepted, gloved with the hope shining
in a child's eyes, for the kiss of tomorrow,
yesterday and today.

Wanda Wuttunee
12 February 2000

Contents

Acknowledgments

The most profound voices in this work are those of the people who took the time to sit with me and share views of their communities that not enough outsiders understand. I honour their kindness, caring, and sharing and sit humbly with them in setting down their words for all of you. They understood that you might learn from their experiences, and so they willingly shared their ways of facing the enormous tasks of governing and nurturing their communities successfully. I have deep gratitude for the privilege of spending time with each person who contributed. This work arose out of a need to answer some questions and to know more about my community. I am grateful for the insights that I can share with you.

Most research projects, like this one, are only good ideas without the support of the funders who choose to be part of the vision. This project enjoyed the support of the Dené Cultural Institute (DCI), Fort Smith, NWT, with the financial backing of Aboriginal Business Canada. I owe a debt of gratitude to Joanne Barnaby, former DCI executive director; DCI's board of directors; and from Aboriginal Business Canada (ABC), Bob Dickson; the Aboriginal Advisory committee; Jay Illingworth and Roger Druin.

Mike Robinson, former executive director of the Arctic Institute of North America, provided support in the beginning of the project, with assistance from Karim Aly-Kassam and Gerry Thompson. Karim's Gwich'in research was very useful, and Gerry's financial finesse was gratefully appreciated. Ernie Daniels (DCI) picked up the financial ball and provided critical assistance.

Technical support for transcribing numerous interviews was provided by Krista Anger, Thelma Gonsalves, Barbara Pritchard, and Nola

Wuttunee. Their assistance was professional and essential to the successful completion of this project.

My family was inextricably bound with this project. Early mornings and weekend work were added to the rhythm of our lives together, and my heart is full with trying to say thanks. Drew is my dancing light, and Cody is an inquisitive, lively young man. Both speak to my heart and give me balance. Trevor is my kind and loving life partner who helps keep it together. I am grateful for their love, the chance to share in their adventures and then to bring some of that energy to my work. The love of all my extended family and friends stretches out to support and guide me in innumerable ways. I give thanks, for I am truly blessed.

The path I have taken in seeking greater understanding has brought me into gentle spheres of influence. I am grateful to the helpers and elders whose wisdom touched me. The sacred fire and love of life burn forever in my heart. Thank you.

Preface

In observing Aboriginal economic development, business, and entrepreneurship growth, the issue of what choices will be made to meet community and individual goals is of paramount interest to me. Will we want communities where the environment is cherished and elders and traditions are honoured, or will we try to maximize returns on investment? Are these objectives mutually exclusive? What does it mean to us to participate meaningfully in the economy? What are the benefits, and what are the costs?

After almost twenty years spent researching and writing in this field, I believe that as Aboriginal people, we can bring something to the table of business. It is something precious, and requires nurturing and awareness: spirit, community, and perspective. Capitalism is seductive in its all pervasiveness and in what it promises to deliver. For Aboriginal communities, blindly following the precepts of capitalism may not provide all the answers or guarantee a standard of living that is meaningful, holistic, and connected to our history. There are scholars in such disparate fields of science, philosophy, and economics who recognize the high costs of development synonymous with the demands for change articulated by sustainable developers, community economic developers, and increasingly, world governments.

As Aboriginal peoples, we may not want to mirror mainstream business choices. We may bring emotion, spirit, and caring in addition to strong business skills. We may choose a package of strategies that in the end provides balance in ways that vary across Aboriginal nations but maintain an integrity not often seen in the business world. Some of us have chosen and more may choose to embrace capitalism wholeheartedly. We all have choices. That is the beauty of the society we live in. I make my choices with my children in mind. I bring my songs into the boardroom as reminders to listen to my heart. If business decision-makers included in every checklist of project efficiency and effectiveness a box to tick off that would minimize negative impacts on our children's quality of life and happiness, the world would be better and business would be better.

The case studies offered in this book provide some insight into communities that are making choices in economic development. They were gathered over a period from 1991 through 1996. Their balance is personal. Their choices commonly honour tradition and community members young and old, while bringing meaning to governance and empowerment. In the urban case study, elements of community are segmented, and each organization examined takes a holistic approach to the extent that this is possible.

Obviously many changes have occurred in these communities since the studies were done. My point is that something can be learned from the particular experiences I captured at the time. Staff have moved on, organizations have closed down, new projects have begun. The Aboriginal perspective, which has unique elements and elements shared in common with world philosophies, is alive and well.

LIVING RHYTHMS

Introduction
Indigenous Economics
Has Values Added

Indigenous economics: the science of dealing with the production, distribution, and consumption of wealth in a naturally holistic, reciprocal manner that respects humankind, fellow species, and the eco-balance of life.
— First Nations Development Institute (FNDI), Virginia, U.S.A.

Truly understanding the essence of economics demanded by the First Nations Development Institute's definition as more than supply and demand invites a shift of perspective in the heart. It requires a connection to spirit that goes beyond the scientific analysis of numbers of jobs created and revenues generated. The scientific-calculation approach commonly employed in the western world begets the measuring tools and sets the standards for "success" that all are meant to aspire to. In a capitalist framework, more is better, and the wonder of capitalism is that the resource supply is endless. These are the values of "growth" that are clutched to the bosom of business, as we know it.

This system finds it difficult to quantify some of the terms in the definition above. What number tells you that you have achieved respect for humankind? What is the value of your care for your fellow species? How do you measure the impact of your actions on the eco-balance of life? The answers to these questions are difficult to address if your only reference point is numbers. People may ignore them altogether as too overwhelming or try to define them to death and squabble with each other over the "best" definition. Thus, little changes, and in the meantime the damage continues.

Indigenous peoples have unique aspirations and worldviews, with threads of understanding and dreams held in common with most of humankind. How do we fit into the aforementioned world of economic development? Do we hold the same aspirations and values as mainstream society? How are they the same, and how are they different? These are the broader questions that you will have some sense of after reading about these Aboriginal communities in western Canada.

WESTERN WORLDVIEWS IN THE CONTEXT OF ECONOMIC DEVELOPMENT

While in the main Aboriginal peoples demonstrate common approaches, as Berkes (1999) notes, individual approaches of communities differ in numerous ways reflecting their particular history and environment (179). These experiences have shaped distinct worldviews in Aboriginal society. The same may be said for mainstream society. The aspects of mainstream worldviews of interest here are the western scientific approach to understanding the world, the way in which values and beliefs have been captured by capitalism, and the accompanying impact on economic development.

In considering worldviews, history is one place to start. The Royal Commission of Aboriginal Peoples (RCAP) has set out a view of history that acknowledges different worldviews and perspectives. In the end, it accords value to differing perspectives held by Euro-Canadians and Aboriginal peoples. For those who disagree or who like to chart the two worldviews side by side and compare them, one Aboriginal scholar points out that it is time to end such meaningless and unfair comparisons (Masuzumi, 1998). Barney Masuzumi notes that one view is no better or worse than the other, but each may complement the other at times. Together they may provide a more accurate view of historical events.

While their approaches to time and history are different, RCAP states that these worldviews are important "not because they represent absolute distinctions between people – cultural worlds are too rich and complex for that – but because they serve to illustrate, however inadequately, that there are different ways of expressing ideas that, at a deeper level, may have much in common" (RCAP, 1996, 1, 35).

Euro-Canadian worldviews are heavily influenced by the western science approach. For example, historians using a western science approach rely on written documentation to support an interpretation of events as a matter of "truth." A cross-cultural setting complicates the strategies for achieving the goal of accurate and "complete" understanding (RCAP, 1996, 1, 32), ruling out oral histories, the basis of Aboriginal "history," as valid information sources.

In accounting for all events under investigation, historians weave their explanations placing human beings at the core in a secular, scientific manner that maintains the split with spirituality advocated through the ages by Galileo, Descartes, Newton, Einstein, and other influential western scientists and philosophers (Lendsay and Wuttunee, 1997, 1) There were no alternative theories and explanations from Aboriginal perspectives until recently, when Aboriginal scholars joined the arena by publishing their perspectives in words that flowed from their various disciplines, oftentimes including a unique Aboriginal view born of personal experience.

The absence of spirituality from the western scientific view of the world and how it works has a major bearing on dominant society's connection to other living things. Objectivity and rigorous documentation are the main tools for discerning meaning and comprehending with logic accurate and reliable answers to questions about how world systems work. This approach has permeated the way research is conducted in many disciplines. The result has been marginalization of the research subjects from the research process. According to Ward (1997), local peoples, including Aboriginal peoples, are viewed as "subjects" in keeping with a scientific or positivist approach to research. She notes that this philosophical framework reflects societal values and beliefs and so accepts positive facts and observable data as appropriate measures of reality (5). In particular, she points to four basic assumptions of positivism:

(1) the aims, concepts and methods of the natural sciences are applicable to the social sciences; (2) the correspondence theory of truth which holds that reality is knowable through correct measurement methods; (3) the goal of social research is to discover universal laws of human behaviour which transcend culture and history; (4) the fact-value dichotomy, the denial of both the theory-laden dimensions of observation and the value-laden dimensions of theory.

This approach to understanding the world and its inhabitants has shaped many academic disciplines. Values, cultures, and spirituality are compartmentalized and have little significance in this scientific aspect of Euro-Canadian worldviews; however, they do have meaning in religion and other non-scientific aspects of our experience.

Nuclear physicist Fritjof Capra, in a more broadly drawn statement of the elements of a dominant worldview held by modern western society,

states that it has become entrenched and influential to the point where
these elements are no longer useful. Indeed, as outlined in the following,
they have become harmful to a productive existence: "The universe is a
mechanical system composed of elementary building blocks; the human
body is a machine; life in society is a competitive struggle for existence;
the belief in unlimited material progress to be achieved through economic and technological growth, and the belief that a society in which
the female is everywhere subsumed by the male is one that follows a basic law of nature" (Capra, 1996: 6).

ROOM FOR IMPROVEMENT:
A PLACE FOR SPIRIT

How are humankind's economic needs met within the context of this
Euro-Canadian worldview? According to David Suzuki (1997), growth
in demand for consumer goods and the continued pursuit of the goals of
capitalism characterized the twentieth century from its beginning. In
1907, economist Simon Nelson Patten espoused the idea that the new
morality consisted in expanding consumption and not in saving. Consumption became the answer for supporting the economy that had
boomed during World War II. Retailing analyst Victor Lebow declared:
"Our enormously productive economy ... demands that we make consumption our way of life, that we convert the buying and use of goods
into rituals, that we seek our spiritual satisfaction, our ego satisfaction,
in consumption ... We need things consumed, burned up, worn out, replaced, and discarded at an ever-increasing rate" (Suzuki, 1997, 21).

Continued growth in consumerism was achieved by identifying new
markets in third world countries, targeting specific groups for products,
and encouraging planned obsolescence. Suzuki observes the "quasi-reli-
gious attitude towards market opportunity" of Coca-Cola president
Donald R. Keough, who said, "When I think of Indonesia – a country on
the Equator with 180 million people, a median age of 18, and with a Mos-
lem ban on alcohol – I feel I know what heaven looks like" (1997, 21).

Governments of all countries and the majority of businesses throughout the world support the rationale for constant growth in consumption
and the economy. McCann, Fullgrabe, and Godfrey-Smith assert that
growth leads to increasing wealth, and this, through the market system,
provides the basis for the satisfaction of all human needs (1984, 35).

What does this philosophy mean for humankind and the limited resources of this planet? Simply put, says Paul Hawken, business is de-

stroying the world. "A hundred years ago, even fifty years ago, it did not seem urgent that we understand the relationship between business and a healthy environment, because natural resources seemed unlimited. Given current corporate practices, not one wildlife reserve, wilderness, or indigenous culture will survive the global market economy" (Hawken, 1993, 3).

The statistics regarding stress, addiction, failing families, and youth at risk in western society indicate that we not happier and healthier as a result of this philosophy of maximum growth for maximum profits. The disconnection from nature and the natural limits of resources is the basis of the push for change in economic development philosophy at all levels. Many authors from varied disciplines are reviewing the facts and suggesting approaches that could mean a difference to future generations.

In my view, a shift must occur away from an approach to economic development that is secular in nature, that is, considers a limited number of issues such as readily quantifiable costs in reaching decisions. We must move instead towards an economic development approach that includes these costs but also attempts to quantify all the costs of development decisions on environment, people, communities, and future generations.

Profit is important as a measure of success, but it is not the only measure. "Reasonable" profit that honours the limits of the planet's resources must replace the idea of "maximum" profit. The guiding principle of maximizing (i.e., develop resources and thereby profit) shifts to moderation (i.e., use resources wisely, and profits will follow) or minimizing (i.e., reduce use of non-renewable resources; develop renewable resources with little long-term residual impact) as the overarching goals of economic activity.

Some business leaders have taken up the cause of rethinking economic development for reasons as diverse as personal revelation, government sanction or regulation, and consumer pressure. Paul Hawken presents an ecological analysis of business in which he argues for business to include environmental perspectives for long-term prosperity. Hawken links a healthy planet with business in an essential partnership that must be nurtured in order to achieve the vision of the future shared by so many people. This is a new era – Ecological Business that follows the Industrial Age (1993, 9).

Hawken urges business leaders to rethink the ultimate purpose of corporations. Rather than focusing on making money and viewing corporations as systems for producing and selling things, common maxims of business behaviour, Hawken suggests that "the promise of business is to increase the general well-being of humankind through service, creative invention and ethical philosophy ... We have the capacity and ability to create a remarkably different economy, one that can restore ecosystems and protect the environment while bringing forth innovation, prosperity, meaningful work, and true security"(1–2).

Hawken acknowledges that in the past the need to understand or recognize any relationship between business and a healthy environment was easily dismissed and the limits on natural resources were ignored because they were not obviously depleting. Today, however, environmental limits to human and industrial activities are a reality, and the hard questions Hawken asks are:

How can business itself survive a continued pattern of worldwide degradation of living systems?

What is the logic of extracting diminishing resources in order to create capital to finance more consumption and demand placed on those diminishing resources?

How do we imagine our future when our commercial systems conflict with everything nature teaches us? (1993, 5).

Hawken sees a productive business environment that will actually *restore* the earth using highly effective organizational and marketing techniques of free enterprise (9). Each partner can learn and benefit from the others. What measures of success become possibilities under this new paradigm? According to Hawken:

The language of commerce sounds specific, but in fact it is not explicit enough. If Hawaiians had 138 different ways to describe falling rain, we can assume that rain had a profound importance in the lives. Business, on the other hand, only has two words for profit – gross and net. The extraordinarily complex manner in which a company recovers profit is reduced to a single numerically neat and precise concept.

It makes no distinctions as to how the profit was made. It does not factor in whether people or places were exploited, resources depleted, communities enhanced, lives lost, or whether the entire executive suite was in such turmoil as to require stress consultants and out placement services for the victims. In other words, business does not discern whether the profit is one of quality or quantity (10).

The most common gauge of success – profit – must now become more holistic in approach, Hawken urges, by reflecting the full value of decisions and acknowledging that business does not exist in a vacuum.

Another common guide for gauging success is a precept that guides business and justifies taking decisions on the narrow basis described by Darwin's "survival of the fittest." According to Hawken, this phrase is actually "a misinterpretation of Darwinism. Darwin did not speak of survival of the fittest; rather, he described those who survived as fittest for a specific ecological niche. There is a big difference between those two ideas ... [Today] the 'winners' are the companies that consistently overstep and exceed carrying capacity. Corporate capitalism recognizes no limit and has no habitat" (33).

It is this attitude of succeeding at all costs that has become too expensive for us and for Mother Earth. According to Hawken, the new corporate "winner" sets reasonable limits on activities and is responsible to many stakeholders in meeting the challenge that he articulates – restoring ecosystems and protecting the environment while being innovative and prosperous in the context of meaningful work.

Most commonly, scale of operations and growth are the foundation for measuring success of today's competitive businesses. Changing the way success is determined when considering the aspirations of sustainable development leads to respect for limits of our physical world and to a healthier way of doing business. Tools are being developed, but so far they are used by very few businesses. Environmental accounting, for example, tries to address some of these issues. It attempts to account for internal and external environmental, economic, and societal costs and benefits. Interdisciplinary in nature, it takes many possible approaches. It may focus on incorporating as a component of product cost "the cost of extracting raw materials, manufacturing, transportation, product recycling, disassembling, reverse distribution, restocking used material, disposing of waste, etc. [A broader approach might be taken where] an assessment is made of the environmental impact of a product or process over its entire life-cycle" (Society of Management Accountants of Canada, 11).

These approaches give hope that some importance is now placed on making standard practices more realistic. A complementary philosophy recognizing the need for change arises from the discipline of economics. According to Daly, an economist, and Cobb, a theologian (1994), "The scale of human activity relative to the biosphere has grown too large ... population has doubled ... Over the same time period, gross world product and fossil fuel consumption have each roughly quadrupled. Further growth beyond the present scale of economic activity is overwhelmingly likely to increase costs more rapidly than it increases benefits, thus ushering in a new era of 'uneconomic growth' that impoverishes rather than enriches" (2).

Other psychologists, economists, and ecologists have come to the same sorts of conclusions (cf. Henderson, 1978; Weiskopf, 1971; Polyani, 1957; Schumpeter, 1975). The goals of maximization of growth, scale of operations, and return on investment must be replaced with that of minimizing throughput while meeting the needs of the human family.

While Hawken seeks to persuade business people to shift their decision-making paradigm, Daly and Cobb seek a similar goal by applying pressure on economists. They suggest an economic perspective that emphasizes "person-in-community" rather than private personal preferences (7–8). "The change will involve correction and expansion, a more empirical and historical attitude ... and the willingness to subordinate the market to purposes that it is not geared to determine"(8). The shift is towards community but without forgetting the needs of the individual.

Daly and Cobb urge a vision that includes human communities and "the other creatures with whom human beings share the world ... the economy that sustains the total web of life and everything that depends on the land" (18). Their vision is personal, and they express it strongly: "At a deep level of our being we find it hard to suppress the cry of anguish, the scream of horror ... We human beings are being led to a dead end – all too literally. We are living by an ideology of death and accordingly we are destroying our own humanity and killing the planet. Even the one great success of the program that has governed us, the attainment of material affluence, is now giving way to poverty ... If we continue on our present path, future generations, if there are to be any, are condemned to misery" (21).

Where organizations follow a policy of sustainability, Daly and Cobb maintain, these organizations must commit to financing projects that are sustainable. They must compare them with other sustainable projects. Where there is exploitation of a nonrenewable resource, there should be a second complementary project that will ensure the sustainability of both projects (74).

The authors caution against using evaluation methods that are not inherently sustainable: for example, using a project discount rate of 5 per cent or less in direct contrast to the usual rates of 15 to 20+ per cent return sought by today's Fortune 500 (75). These 15 to 20 per cent rates of return are inflated because all relevant costs of production are not included. When all costs are included, then the rate of return is adjusted to a more realistic 5 per cent. They contend that success then becomes a measure that takes into account the impact on the environment, resources, and the quality of living for this generation and future generations.

Researchers in other disciplines who are trying to understand the impact of attitudes on the future of life on Mother Earth are also arriving at similar conclusions. Fritjof Capra opens his book *The Web of Life* with a quotation that has long been attributed to Aboriginal peoples:

> This we know.
> All things are connected
> like the blood
> which unites one's family ...
>
> Whatever befalls the earth,
> befalls the sons and daughters of the earth.
> Man did not weave the web of life;
> he is merely a strand in it.
> Whatever he does to the web,
> he does to himself
> (Ted Perry, inspired by Chief Seattle, quoted in Capra 1996)

Capra attempts to outline an emerging theory of living systems that offers a unified view of mind, matter, and life. Like Hawken and Daly and Cobb, he is moving from a mechanistic to an ecological worldview that has profound implications for "science and philosophy, but also for business, politics, health care, education, and everyday life"(3). He views all major problems of environmental concern as interconnected and interdependent.

A grass-roots movement begun in the early 1970s called "deep ecology" best captures Capra's underlying philosophy of his proposed living system's theory. Deep ecology places all living things on the same level and ascribes equal value, as compared to views that are human centred with nature as merely a tool with little intrinsic value. "Deep ecology recognizes the intrinsic value of all living beings and views humans as just one particular strand in the web of life. Ultimately, deep ecological awareness is spiritual or religious awareness." This is a perspective with much in common with Aboriginal worldviews.

In trying to separate values from facts, science has influenced politics, economics, and social structures in ways that are becoming life destroying rather than life preserving (11). Now, deep ecology encourages a new reality where life is at the very centre.

Capra predicts that with this proposed shift in paradigm, many changes will occur. For example, private profits are currently being made at public cost to the quality of the environment, the general quality of life, and to future generations. "A major clash between economics and ecology derives from the fact that nature is cyclical, whereas our industrial systems are linear. Our businesses take resources, transform them into products plus waste, and sell the products to consumers, who discard more waste when they have consumed the products. Sustainable patterns of production and consumption need to be cyclical, imitating the cyclical processes in nature" (299).

Hawken and Daly and Cobb also reach this conclusion, as do many other noted researchers in different fields. For example, David Suzuki notes that science has proven without a doubt that devastation has occurred and will continue to occur without each person getting involved in the changes that make sense. It has become a personal choice (Rosborough, 1997, D6).

Current research suggests that there is room for a shift in values and approaches to economic development. Aboriginal economic development has common features with the western approach to business for a variety of reasons. Basic elements of earning a reasonable return on investment may be learned and practised by anyone regardless of ethnicity. The way in which Aboriginal society defines "good business practices and standards," for example, is a function of currently held values and traditions. These may be any blend on a spectrum of traditional and capitalist values.

Room for these approaches has not been made by the business establishment, where the common attitude is that "business," "success," "strategies" are the same for all Canadians. Those employees, customers, partners, or colleagues who hold different personal values must not allow them to interfere with proper business conduct if they are to participate or succeed.

Each Aboriginal individual or community carries its own bundle of values and practices that blend western and Aboriginal perspectives in unique ways that are carried to the workplace, in whole or in part. When Aboriginal persons are employed in "mainstream" business, the choice may well be to leave some of their values at the door of the employer, do their business, and pick up their bundle on the way out. While this decision is respectful of the owner and the lodge (place of business) that they are entering, in the long term, the cost to personal beliefs may be too great.

LIVING WITH THE LAND OR OFF THE LAND?

Capra notes a link to the underlying traditions of Aboriginal peoples with the concept of deep ecology. What do Aboriginal peoples contribute to the discussion of sustainable development? There is a connection to the land that the traditions held by many Aboriginal peoples maintain, and there is a different tradition that has evolved for western society that now includes sustainable development. Understanding perspectives that might be characterized as living with the land or as living off of the land is critical. These perspectives cross many boundaries, as illustrated in preceding examples.

A respectful relationship to the land and all living creatures is integrated into the lifestyle of those Aboriginal peoples who are raised with or have regained traditional values. This relationship is characterized by responsibility and thankfulness for all creatures with life in the animate and inanimate worlds, in the sky, deep into the planet and the sun and the moon. This complexity is reached for in Aboriginal languages with a depth of meaning that cannot be adequately expressed or fully translated into English. Spirit, emotion, and mental and physical facets of this relationship are captured in stories, oral traditions of teachers and elders, and through living and experiencing the teachings. Thought is given to the lessons learned from seven generations earlier and the impact their choices will have on the next seven generations.

As with all things, the way this knowledge is held varies from Aboriginal person to person. Some are able to express traditional values each day of their lives, while some have been assimilated, perhaps from living in the city for several generations, and have lost this type of connection as a source of responsibility to Mother Earth. Some have accepted Christianity into their lives, and their values no longer reflect the traditional worldview. Alternatively, their beliefs may still coincide with traditional values despite external influences.

Others are being resensitized, like many Canadians, to the damage that is being done to the planet and have a new link with the land. Still others have traditional values that they are not able to demonstrate because of community pressure for economic development, revenues, and employment benefits. Options damaging to the Earth Mother may be the only type of economic development opportunities that exist for some of these communities, and short-term trade-offs must be made.

Historically, Aboriginal peoples needed to be keen observers of Nature's cycles in order to survive a harsh climate and limited resources. They became masterful at adapting their lifestyle to match these rhythms. For many groups, their oral history reveals the spirituality inherent in their early lifestyle. During the hearings of the Royal Commission on Aboriginal Peoples, many representations were made regarding past and continuing connections to the Earth Mother and what it means to have no control over the damage being done to her in our own backyards (see RCAP, 1996, vols. 1, 2, and 4). There is no question that land plays an important part in the health and future of the Aboriginal community, as it has done in the past. Community members and summaries based on RCAP testimony and research that are echoed in communities across the country capture this significance:

We lived a nomadic lifestyle, following the vegetation and hunting cycles throughout our territory for over 10,000 years. We lived in harmony with the earth, obtaining all our food, medicines and materials for shelter and clothing from nature. We are the protectors of our territory, a responsibility handed to us from the Creator. Our existence continues to centre on this responsibility.

> Denise Birdstone, St Mary's Indian Band,
> Cranbrook, British Columbia,
> 3 November 1992

Aboriginal peoples have told us of their special relationship to the land and its resources. This relationship, they say, is both spiritual and material, not only one of livelihood, but of community and indeed of the continuity of their cultures and societies.

Many Aboriginal languages have a term that can be translated as "land"... To Aboriginal peoples, land has a broad meaning, covering the environment, or what ecologists know as the biosphere, the earth's life-support system. Land means not just the surface of the land, but the subsurface, as well as the rivers, lakes (and in winter, ice), shorelines, the marine environment and the air. To Aboriginal peoples, land is not simply the basis of livelihood but of life and must be treated as such.

The way people have related to and lived on the land (and in many cases continue to) also forms the basis of society, nationhood, governance and community. Land touches every aspect of life: conceptual and spiritual views; securing food, shelter and clothing; cycles of economic activities including the division of labour; forms of social organization such as recreational and cere-monial events; and systems of governance and management.

To survive and prosper as communities, as well as fulfil the role of steward assigned to them by the Creator, Aboriginal societies needed laws and rules that could be known and enforced by their citizens and institutions of gover-nance. This involved appropriate standards of behaviour (law) governing indi-viduals and the collective ... although foreign to and different from the European and subsequent Canadian systems of law and governance – were valid in their own right and continue to be worthy of respect.

Our survival depended on our wise use of game and the protection of the en-vironment. Hunting for pleasure was looked upon as wasteful and all hunters were encouraged to share food and skins. Sharing and caring for all members of the society, especially the old, the disabled, the widows, and the young were the important values of the Mi'kmaq people. Without these values, my people would not have survived for thousands of years as a hunting, fishing and gath-ering culture.

> Kep'tin John Joe Sark,
> Micmac Grand Council,
> Charlottetown, Prince Edward Island,
> 5 May 1992

Even today, Aboriginal peoples strive to maintain this connection between land, livelihood and community. For some, it is the substance of everyday life; for others, it has been weakened as lands have been lost or access to resources [has been] disrupted. For some, the meaning of that relationship is much as it was for generations past; for others, it is being rediscovered and reshaped. *Yet the maintenance and renewal of the connection between land, livelihood, and community remain priorities for Aboriginal peoples everywhere in Canada – whether in the far north, the coastal villages, the isolated boreal forest commu-nities, the prairie reserves and settlements, or in and around the major cities* (emphasis added) (RCAP, 1996, vol. 2, 448–9).

In summary, a traditional Aboriginal worldview respects the land and all life. The lessons of observation and experience embody Aboriginal wisdom relied on for survival for thousands of years (Ghostkeeper, 1997). The rules governing the community required respect, sharing amongst members, and caring for the young and helpless. Celebrating and giving thanks for Creator's gifts were commonly observed when starting the day, for a successful hunt, and in marking many social as-pects of life including coming of age, women's and men's ceremonies, community celebrations, and deaths. The relationship with the land is complex and not easily explained nor experienced for people not born into that tradition. While the tradition continues, it is also changing, as is the wisdom that is relied on to survive in a modern world with its new demands. In today's world, many influences and experiences mean that only a proportion of Aboriginal peoples live with the land and maintain that sacred connection.

When Aboriginal peoples refer to their connection to the land, meaning all living things, a spiritual connection and legacy, they are referring to some of the same things that scholars consider in examining sustainable development and the resources it seeks to manage (Berkes, 1999). The more specific insights you will be offered in this book have to do with accepting an invitation to get to know some dedicated people with experiences to share. They come from all walks of life, and the common feeling that binds them is the desire to improve their communities for their families and friends. All are dedicated to trying, and each has hope that the challenge will be met. Each demonstrates a distinctive barometer of "success." Their goals are coloured by their tradition, respect for the land, and celebration of their own communities.

A STORY OF HOPE

This is not a story of dysfunction and despair. I do not ignore these aspects, for they are woven into the fabric of community life; they are also the subject of extensive study and debate elsewhere. Illness and social problems have impact on economic development because they often mean that good people are unavailable for the rigours of making a living. The profiles of these communities include hard lessons, but they also celebrate the things that are working. No matter how minor it might seem to outsiders, one person trying to make a better life is a triumph and a success.

I interviewed many people in each community over a five-year period – elected leaders, managers, elders, young people, and life givers. They shared so much, and I am very honoured. My purpose has been to understand their economic development strategies for myself and to share that little bit of my understanding with other Aboriginal scholars, leaders, economic developers, and communities as well as with Canadian communities, business people, and corporations. I have shaped this work around the sound of community people's voices describing their experiences. I offer my own insights to generate discussion and build understanding.

Canadian society does not often think of Aboriginal peoples in these terms of independence, contribution, and hope, so I expose the bright lights that are shining in our communities. The benefits of sharing these experiences filter out from our communities to the rest of Canadian society. What can we learn from Aboriginal peoples today about the original reciprocity of sharing and caring that existed when the first European explorer arrived on Turtle Island (North America)? With extensive community damage colouring the lives of many Aboriginal families, news of approaches that are making a difference will inspire more stories of success.

For those whose practices of ignoring the natural limits on resources are the antithesis of traditional respect and use of the land to support communities forever, rethinking the limits of sensible economic development is timely. As we have seen, scholars in different disciplines as diverse as physics, philosophy, ecology, and business are arriving at the same conclusions. Environmental lobby groups are as persistent as ever. For Aboriginal and Canadian business people who think that "success" can only be found by mirroring the poor choices of exploitative development made to date, these selected Aboriginal communities offer alternatives. My unpublished dissertation at the University of Manitoba looks into these issues in greater depth. It is entitled "Economic Development in Selected Aboriginal Communities: Lessons in Strength, Resilience and Celebration," and can be obtained through inter-library loan.

I invite you to "hear" the experiences that follow. Absorb the printed word not only with your intellect but also with your heart. I hope that you gain a meaningful understanding of the challenges and joys facing these Aboriginal communities. The majority are rural; some have access to resources through land claims, while others are in the process of negotiation. Some communities have few natural resources or no access to them. There are several urban examples too. Their lessons are important, but they share a feeling that there are no cookie-cutter solutions. Each experience has shaped the community who owns it. Others are welcome to pick up what is relevant and ask themselves how an idea or strategy might fit in their community. There are no panaceas here. There are the sounds of happiness, the glitter of shining eyes filled with hope, laughter in the face of sadness and pain, and the quietness of the Earth Mother's heartbeat. These are shining lights from various parts of western Canada.

I

Measuring Our Success
in Our Own Way

Common challenges face the Aboriginal communities in this study: high unemployment, poor technical and training skills, health and social dysfunction, and for some, restrictions on control of their land and resources. Several have land claims settlements or are in the process of settling them. For the urban-based community and organizations that were examined, land is not a current issue. The will and hope of the people drive the leadership to continue to forge ahead despite the obstacles.

At St Theresa Point in Manitoba, Chief Mason faces 75 to 80 per cent unemployment, little access to resources, and a stalled land-claims process. The Neeginan project in Winnipeg has for the most part shifted the focus from internal political strife to a positive project that will benefit many Aboriginal peoples. Chief Mack and Chief Frank are involved in lengthy negotiations for Nuu-chah-nulth land claims that take limited human resources away from the other issues that are critical to the communities. Chief Beaver in Alberta has to be vigilant and aggressive with companies that come onto their lands to harvest Bigstone Cree Nation resources without working with their community. These are only a few of the challenges these communities face. The question is: How are these challenges resolved?

For some leaders, the advice of their elders is critical. Toquaht and Tla-o-qui-aht First Nations note the importance of their hereditary chiefs. Tsuu T'ina Nation has an elders advisory committee, as do many of the organizations examined in Winnipeg. The other important guide is the community, and all of these communities and organizations have the processes in place to include meaningful community discussion in making economic development decisions.

Tsuu T'ina Nation has developed its own unique administrative structure that builds on its experience. Winnipeg's Aboriginal community has a number of unique projects that focus positive attention on Aboriginal people and their traditions as well as centralizing many services. Toquaht First Nation has never had an Indian Act election for its leader. There is tradition and entrepreneurial spirit in this community. Tla-o-qui-aht First Nation has a major tourism attraction in its hotel which is a great example of success. The Gwich'in, the only community with land claims, are moving to steward this resource for future generations. They developed an investment strategy using more than sixty community people and revisited it again in order to make changes. Making partnerships work to the benefit of all parties is not an easy task. St Theresa Point and Bigstone Cree Nation are diligent in working at this process.

When asked what success in economic development means, some in these communities noted that increased employment was important – something that could be quantified. More often than not, they judged success in terms of how self-governing they are. External interference is kept to a minimum in some communities, like Tsuu T'ina, or it is a goal tied to control of their lands, as noted by St Theresa Point. Some communities are able to live self-governance now while others feel the weight of the federal government. Small businesses, jobs, education, and training are the priorities for these communities to ensure their continued existence.

Some Aboriginal scholars have examined the area of Aboriginal economic development or indigenous economics. I find the "Elements of Development" model to be of particular interest to this discussion. First Nations Development Institute (FNDI), an Aboriginal-controlled organization, developed this model as a planning tool and starting point for evaluating the impact of development projects through an Aboriginal lens. What is the impact of this perspective on the way successful development is measured in these communities?

THE ELEMENTS OF DEVELOPMENT MODEL

Most economic development theories want to count success by "jobs created, incomes increased, loans made, people trained, houses built, goods and services produced." But those measures cover only a part of the picture. How are impacts on community values, traditions, and perspectives measured?

FNDI has produced a model that is holistic in its approach. The Elements of Development model offers an alternative to the usual approaches to "fixing" undeveloped Aboriginal economies. The usual "problems" of inadequate infrastructures, an unskilled labour force, lack of access to capital, and political instability contrast with an indigenous perspective of what constitutes relevant community strengths.

Historical approaches to the development of Aboriginal communities have commonly devalued them as culture, values, and community institutions or labelled them as obstacles to economic development "success." Alternatively, community economic development (CED) approaches acknowledge community perspectives and attempt to work them into community plans. CED approaches can be effective where skilled practitioners who are open to different definitions of success facilitate the process.

Salway Black (1994) examines several models in the context of Aboriginal economic development. For example, the "Indian Entrepreneur Model" nurtures the profit-oriented focus of a select group within a community. Unfortunately there is no basis for interconnections and the support that a local economic system on a reserve requires, and usually these individuals go to markets that are more lucrative (10). Another example, the "Chamber of Commerce Model of Development," sees success in attracting outside industry to the community. The drawbacks for the community in this case include continued reliance on outside interests that neither take minimal responsibility for community welfare nor are particularly accountable. Both of these examples ignore indigenous worldviews about economic development.

Effective economic development strategies for Aboriginal communities recognize the need for strong leadership that understands and supports local needs. They recognize a kinship system which is not duplicated in western society, and they have room for many cultural values.

Salway Black's work identifies a number of areas contributing to dependency in a reserve economy and stresses that these findings must be recognized in developing a more relevant perspective:

• Within each Native community, there are household income generating activities, self-help efforts and other untapped and idle resources that can be mobilized for successful economic development.
• An empowered Native economy can develop "win-win" partnerships with the surrounding economies; leverage resources; build strong networks with Na-

tive development; and enhance existing markets as well as develop new markets based on community knowledge of what people need.
• Organizational or group activities, modified to generate revenues, can decrease dependency on federal funds and increase the capacity for planning, initiating, managing, and marketing development activities
• A diversified local economy decreases the flow of money out of the community, promoting local recirculation of money, which enhances continued development.
• Economic development must start with the people. It is about leadership, vision and the right to a dignified livelihood for all people. (12)

This approach focuses on balance, which is also taught in the Cree Medicine Wheel's physical, spiritual, emotional, and mental coordinates. Communities can modify this tool so that it is appropriate to their individual values, beliefs, and culture.

The Elements of Development model, noted in figure 1, is made up of circles within circles. The circle is "an important symbol in Native American society, demonstrating the interconnection of all things and the balance of life. The circle is useful to demonstrate an holistic model by visually indicating that we cannot look at parts of the whole, but must examine the entire picture" (Salway Black, 1994, 14).

This symbol acknowledges values, history, culture, and tradition as all important. The interior circles, starting from the centre and going outwards, represent the individual, the project, the community, and the national Aboriginal populace. The figure is divided into four, with each axis representing a major relationship in economic development, in particular, spirituality, kinship, personal efficacy, and asset control.

Within each quadrant there are three elements of the economic development process, for a total of sixteen elements that guide the goal setting and evaluation processes (FNDI, 1994, 14). The element of spirituality is a critical part of economic development for Aboriginal peoples. In this context, it most strongly reflects an Aboriginal perspective where a vision of oneself, one's place in the community and in the rest of creation, is the starting point. This vision is a context for understanding economic development choices. Connections are made with values, all living things, respect, dignity, and the place for Aboriginal peoples in the world. Spirituality is difficult to measure as a part of successful economic development, but some indicators might include "instilling traditional teachings in the children, learning the language, creating visions for the future, recognizing and maintaining a balance in life. For the community ... spirituality can be measured by ... cultural

Figure 1. Elements of Development Model

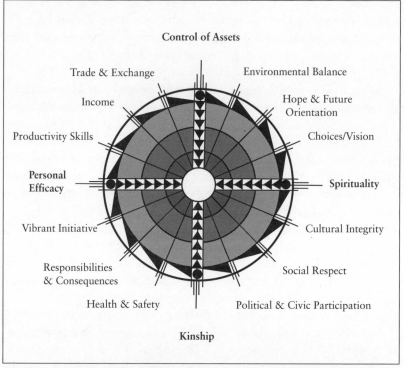

From *Redefining Success in Community Development: A New Approach for Determining and Measuring the Impact of Development*, S. Salway Black, Shramm Paper on Community Development: The Lincoln Filene Centre. Copyright 1994 by the First Nations Development Institute. Reprinted with permission

programs, traditional methods and teachings that both empower and develop people" (FNDI, 1994, 17).

For many Aboriginal people, their source of spirituality is the Bible, and this diversity is also honoured in this model.

The next major element, kinship, acknowledges the system of "giving, sharing and reciprocity" that exists within Aboriginal communities despite the western-based models of distribution that are also practised. By acknowledging and building on the kinship system, a strategy builds on local strengths. Indicators would include acknowledging a family's activities in meeting local needs with local resources and further trade activities within communities and between communities (17).

Self-confidence, or personal efficacy, is next on the circle for Elements of Development. Individual achievements and accomplishments are honoured when they benefit the extended family and community.

Children are taught about self-confidence, risk taking, innovation, and experience, so that the community continues to grow in effectiveness and efficiency. Growth for its own sake is not valued. From an early age, children are taught to "think for yourself and act for others." This approach creates a respect for others that western society has interpreted as noncompetitiveness.

Indicators of improvement in personal efficacy include increased knowledge, skills, self-confidence, problem-solving abilities, and positive attitudes. Indicators at a community level may include better leadership, community cooperation, reliability, follow-up, and teamwork. On a national level, a positive attitude for achievement permeates Aboriginal society (17).

Finally, control of assets is an essential element of economic development that salutes empowerment through ownership and control, enabling wealth creation. According to Salway Black, an individual's assets can be a house, a savings account, an education, job skills, traditional rights to hunt, a business, and access to credit. Similarly, a community's assets may be programs, land, indigenous institutions, environmental quality, trust funds, traditional hunting rights, access to credit, and natural and human resources. At the national level for tribes, assets are trust funds, federal programs, their own indigenous institutions, and sovereignty (16).

The quadrant in the Elements of Development that is delineated by kinship and spirituality includes the elements of *political and civic participation* (e.g., involvement in community activities), *social respect* (e.g., public involvement for better policies and improved media coverage about Aboriginal peoples), and *cultural integrity* (e.g., passing down of traditional language and culture). Salway Black suggests this quadrant captures demonstration of empowerment and personal and societal understanding (18).

Kinship and personal efficacy form a quadrant that includes *vibrant initiative* (e.g., entrepreneurship, self-confidence, self-esteem, and creativity), *responsibilities and consequences* (e.g., with ownership and control come responsibility and accountability to yourself and to the community), and *health and safety* (e.g., reflecting local priorities, and partnerships tied to kinship, community, and health practitioners) (18).

Personal efficacy and assets include elements of *trade and exchange* (e.g., are dollars recirculating in the community or leaving?), *income* (sources of income for community members), and *productivity* (skill levels in formal and informal community activities). While these are

most similar to conventional economic measures, this section expands
to include informal trade and barter. It would also include an expanded
definition of employment that integrates cultural sensitivity. Employment options do not stop at wage labour but go beyond to include a
dignified livelihood (17–18).

The final quadrant denoted by spirituality and assets includes
choices/vision (e.g., do people feel they have choices? what are they?),
hope and future orientation (personal or mission statements that note
the effect of today's actions on the future), and *environmental balance*
(e.g., water, air, and soil quality, improved waste management systems,
and integrated resource management programs based on traditional
practices) (18–19).

It is important to understand the context. This model operates
within the limits of the Earth Mother. Development does not dominate,
nor is it separate so the model is depicted as enfolded within "ecology."

This model, with its gift of new types of indicators, brings another
dimension to the discussion of community-based economic development and strategies for nurturing Aboriginal economies. Salway Black
observes, as do other scholars, that most programs for Aboriginal peoples encourage them to enter the very market-based, capitalist system
that has marginalized many of them for years. Many Aboriginal business leaders are completely comfortable in the capitalist system and are
very successful in terms of the dollars they earn. This alternative approach, however, strives for a balance and additional terms of reference
that may be picked up by anyone and used to modify or direct their approaches to development. Relationships between people, communities,
and environment with a spiritual underpinning are honoured and are
the focus for economic development within a context of values, culture,
and tradition. Many of these factors were labelled as problems or ignored in the regular approach to business and economic development.
Now they form the basis for success.

FNDI operates an economic development fund for use by individuals
and communities. The Elements of Development guide FNDI in assessing requests. Business plans are produced using this model as a basis.
The model is modified to suit the needs and aspirations of applicants in
concert with FNDI staff. Between 1993 and 1996 grants totalling more
than $4 million were made in support of ninety-nine projects that in-
cluded culture and beliefs (FNDI 1996/97, 45).

FNDI's rationale for new economic development indicators is complex
and provides the basis for a reassessment or validation for a different

approach to "success." Local community involvement in setting goals and evaluation of goals is empowering. These indicators may serve as catalysts for change through all levels of society. Local values, goals, and priorities are set without interference from outside sources. Indicators that examine all kinds of impacts can be documented for justifying further investment. A holistic approach is more meaningful for many Aboriginal communities, helping to clarify the future vision and creating a new paradigm of economic development (Salway Black, 1994, 23). Specifically, "indicators register increases in civic participation and proactive decision making, income streams within and around the community, assumption of responsibility by community members, and various intangibles such as self-esteem and sense of cultural identity" (FNDI 1996/97, 46).

This approach includes all living things and is the starting point for a new discussion on broader issues of impacts caused by entering into the market economy. Capitalism has many aspects, and some of these aspects may not be what Aboriginal communities define as part of their vision. With FNDI's approach, Aboriginal peoples have tools to begin to journey on their own path, drawing on knowledge from all sources in crafting their visions for the future. This model is not restricted for use by communities, organizations, or individuals who live on reserves or in rural settings. The approach can support any project, including ones located in an urban setting.

Gathering community members together to consider each axis allows use of this model as a planning tool. Assuming the centre is valued at zero and the end of the axis is ten, indicating how strong a community is on that axis, a group can plot the community profile on each axis. By joining the points, the shape of their community will emerge. A circle indicates balance in all four quadrants. If the same exercise is repeated after a project is completed, then the shape will change providing a means for monitoring change. It can also be the basis for setting community objectives, particularly if some are points on the axes could be stronger. For example, the community may want to focus on developing its kinship systems or dealing with hope and future visioning.

It is important to begin using our own ways of looking at the world and at our communities based on our needs. We may draw on the model of capitalism, but there are many things that communities may want to do in their own ways. This model is one tool, but more must be developed. It is a partnership with benefits for everyone.

The following chapters offer the particular perspectives of people who are inextricably linked to their Aboriginal communities in Canada today. The final chapter sets some of their experiences within the context of the Elements of Development model and provides the basis for further discussion in communities across this country. For example, partnerships illustrate the benefits and challenges of working at strong business relationships. These are worthwhile when community weaknesses can be balanced with a partner's strengths. The Tribal Councils Investment Group (TCIG) is an excellent example of a partnership run in a business-like fashion, generating income that goes back to communities to spend on whatever their priorities are, including projects that support culture and tradition.

Our young people need to be nurtured for their future roles. Many quit school early and later come back for training, since "you can only watch so much TV." They may need that break, but if opportunities can hook them when they are ready, then the community has a better chance. Tsuu T'ina provides opportunities for their young people to apprentice on their major projects with outside consultants or experienced staff, identifying and building on strengths with the input and guidance of the young people themselves. The young people are involved and committed to the future with the community. Aboriginal Youth With Initiative (AYWI) is an excellent example of our young people's drive. They love sharing ideas with other groups.

Business can learn from the experiences of these potential partners and from companies and communities who are successfully partnering. Working together takes sensitivity, commitment, and a holistic view of being in business. It is more than profit. I invite every corporate executive, leader, and manager to imagine this scenario: Just before you make a decision that will affect another person, a family, community, nation, or future generations, close your eyes and bring a child that you love into your thoughts. Imagine looking into those eyes when you announce your decision.

IN CLOSE PROXIMITY

2

Tsuu T'ina Nation, Alberta

TSUU T'INA NATION is located literally across the street in South Calgary. Chief Roy Whitney is facilitating the successful development of his community. Their many projects include band owned businesses developing the limited natural resources they own, offering services, managing a premium housing development, and running several golf courses. They have a business park and lease space to a variety of companies in their administration building. The community has strong attachments to the land and the needs of the people. They have learned many hard lessons. In this community, balancing politics and business is a fine art.

Tsuu T'ina people, who are Athabascan, are related to Dene in the north and Navajo in the south. A story is told of a serpent monster that lived under the ice where Athabascan people were crossing:

It had a horn on its head and a small piece of horn was sticking out of the ice. A grandmother was carrying a child on her back. The child saw that horn and began crying for it. Half of the people were already across the ice and the other half were just getting onto the ice.

The child's grandmother started chipping away at the horn in order to stop the child from crying. She awoke the serpent monster with the vibration of the chipping. The monster stood up and broke the ice and separated the people. Many people perished including the child and grandmother. Similar stories are told but the Navajo talk of a buffalo and the Dene from the Northwest Territories say it was an elk horn. (Hal Eagletail, 1994)

The theme of separation and independence continues when, after the signing of Treaty Seven in 1877, Chief Bullhead (Chula) moved his people

north to the place where the reserve is currently located on 27,600 hectares, on the southeast edge of Calgary, Alberta. Chief Roy Whitney
(1994, personal communication) says, "If we were to survive, we had to
survive as our own people. Chief Bullhead fought for this area as a location for our First Nation, and that's how we settled here."

A prophecy was made when the Tsuu T'ina people moved and a new
marker was placed claiming new reserve lands. A medicine warrior
named Eagleribs said he saw boxes surrounding this reserve in the future. Boxes were building themselves around the community. He said
that this was going to be an opportunity and would be the time for the
community to teach the people building the boxes about the Nation.
According to Hal Eagletail (1994, personal communication), "We were
to support ourselves with them as customers, through economic development. Several portions of reserve boundary lie across the street from
Calgary homes – the boxes."

Surviving in their settlement was a challenge. When the treaty was
signed, there were 1,500 members. Disease had decimated the community by the 1930s, leaving 170 survivors. Chief Roy Whitney
(1994, personal communication) describes the way the elders
advised this challenge to their survival be met: "Our old people got
together and said our people were to start marrying now if we were
to survive as a people. That's when our people started marrying into
other tribes. The men brought the families back, and the women
went with their husbands and left to go to the other tribes. There is
quite a mixture now and in some places we were called the 'united
nations.' We have seventy-nine people that speak the Athabascan di-
alect, the Dene tongue. We are working to incorporate it into our
school and into our administration."

The elders' instructions saved the community. Of a total of 1,300
members in 1996, approximately 920 lived on the reserve (Indian
and Northern Affairs, 1999). Five hundred were less than eighteen
years of age, and sixty were above the age of fifty-five years. This
left four hundred Nation members available for employment. According to Peter Manywounds, commissioner for Business and Development (1994, personal communication), the unemployment rate
was approximately 6 per cent when all projects were fully operational. This rate fluctuated throughout the year because some work
was seasonal.

In 1996 the following statistics set the educational profile of those
members who were fifteen years or older. Of those members with grade

nine or higher, 57 per cent had graduated from high school. Of the 26 per cent with some non-university training, 81 per cent held a certificate or diploma. Of the 37 per cent membership who had university training, 65 per cent held a bachelor's degree or higher (Indian and Northern Affairs website, 1999).

Band-owned projects include a gravel company, a housing development called Redwood Meadows, and a small gas well project. A business park, golf course, explosive device disposal company, and construction projects such as several schools, an elders' residence, and an office complex provide more employment for Nation members.

Tsuu T'ina Nation follows the advice of its elders and leaders. They essentially govern themselves in all ways and all times, but like other First Nations (for example, Sakgeeng First Nation, Manitoba), do not speak in terms of "self-government." The elders counsel against speaking about self-government because the way they understand that term does not coincide with the way it is used by the federal government. It is not necessary to speak of that term because the Nation leads the way quietly by developing by-laws and other legislation to guide development on their lands, on their terms.

Darrell Crowchild, chief commissioner for Tsuu T'ina Nation (1994, personal communication), describes his understanding of his community's perspective and self-government:

We look at self-government from the perspective of a traditional government. Decisions and the ways decisions are made aren't all written down. Now we're taking the next step and writing it down.

We looked at self-government a few years ago when the federal government brought it forward. Almost all the First Nations were scrambling in a sense and talking about membership codes and self-government. We've gotta grab onto something and protect ourselves. I looked on it as almost a tactic that the federal government used against the Indian people to get them to give in to a way of protecting themselves or their Nations. I thought that it would lead to a breakdown of barriers but we would become weak. Dangle dollars and programs in front of our faces so that we jump.

I think that the only way that is ever going to work is if we define it for ourselves and with sense and respect for other communities. It won't work to have one definition for all communities across Canada.

As with many communities, social problems exist, and the community is working to solve them. People must be healthy for development initiatives to succeed. According to elder Rose Runner (1994, personal communication):

My heart gets very heavy when I think about the community and what is going on. There is violence in the homes, personal problems, and people are crying out for help and people are not hearing it.

What I tell my children is that "You are very important. You are uniquely made and the Heavenly Father made you so special that you are not like anyone else in this whole world. You are priceless and your life is priceless. Deal with your life first and look at yourself before you help your family."

It is up to the individual to work on themselves and to think about their families first before they try and help others. I don't think you can help anybody if you are not helping yourself. You know, you gotta find a peace within you before you can learn to give it.

ECONOMIC DEVELOPMENT

A community with a vision has direction and can articulate a path to accomplish its goals. For Tsuu T'ina Nation, the goal in 1994 was to move away from dependence on government. The main strategy was to heal community members and develop economically viable projects that earned revenue and provided employment. They wanted their young people to work in the community in positions with a future.

Comments by key decision-makers follow, and include the community's chief, a councillor holding the economic development portfolio, the chief commissioner, and the manager of economic development. They provide insight and glimpses into the personal vision guiding each of them.

ADMINISTRATION

Chief Roy Whitney has held his position since 1986. He believes in all aspects of the community: social, cultural, traditional, and familial. He comments on the process (1994, personal communication) and the goal for economic development:

Any development or program that we have started, I have always ensured that we go back to the old people first and we start with prayer to ensure it has the cultural and traditional strength. They will say this is what you should watch for and gear towards for the future. Any new adventure we begin that way, and we involve the old people at the very beginning. It's really important to the community.

Our main goal is to be self-sustaining. We want to rely solely on ourselves and as a First Nation to meet the needs of this community. We want to create jobs and supporting infrastructure. We tell our young people to seek an education that will create independence and self-esteem. They can come back to this community and know that there is a job or potential for a job waiting for them.

Self-sustainability is not self-government, but it will give our next generation the ability to make decisions on the needs of their own community. They will use financial resources that are made available to them from this community.

Steve Runner is council member and holds the Economic Development portfolio. He is a successful rancher who echoes Whitney's concern for young people and the need to generate revenue to achieve independence. He calls for balance in bringing all the community together to enjoy the results. In his view there are many other issues (1994, personal communication) still to be addressed:

Our members have money in their pockets, but at the same time, social problems are not being dealt with. We have to slow down and deal with these problems. We have had many deaths among the young people from alcohol-related accidents and from suicide.

Other challenges that face our community include the proximity to Calgary. It can be positive due to economic development opportunities, but it also means that drugs and alcohol are close. Further, the City of Calgary ties us up with their plans to use some of our land. For example, they wanted to build a highway bypass, and they negotiated for three years. We had environmental and cultural studies done, and in the end it held us up for eight years.

Darrell Crowchild (1994, personal communication) is a member who has lived a traditional lifestyle from a young age. He brings that perspective and values to the community that he has worked in for most of his adult life.

The future of our community is an issue that has been talked about for a number of years by staff and council. Where is the Nation going to be in ten years, twenty years, or forty years down the road? How are we going to get there?

Our biggest issue is looking at our own people. What skills and education do we possess in the community? What is needed for our people to enter into business arrangements? How do we get the majority of our own people actually running businesses, programs, and projects? If we require outside expertise, then we must bring these people in, but have training in place so Tsuu T'ina Nation people are running the whole show in the end.

In order to answer these questions and reach our goal, we put all the projects we had on the table. We tried to identify where we need to improve education and training levels for our youth and adults so we could best utilize our people for the Nation's operations.

We looked at upgrading education levels, established a committee, and within four months we put together a whole plan. The upgrading program was running by September that year. Thirty people joined the upgrading program. Within a month we were up to sixty people, and we capped enrolment.

Key people in social services, education, economic development, and employment formed a committee to help develop the upgrading program. A coordinator was hired who handles regular negotiations with Mount Royal College, the University of Lethbridge, and the University of Calgary for direct purchase of programs.

Next we invite our young people to apply for jobs with the Nation's programs and companies. They are matched with experienced personnel and receive training and guidance so they succeed. We give them opportunities to learn about the Nation and its operations, to work with various Nation members and companies, which gives them encouragement.

There have been wonderful turn-around stories in our people who are now inspired to become part of the Nation's workforce. They want to contribute to the Nation as a whole. There are now peer role models who inspire other young people to work hard and join the Nation's vision. It's very exciting.

Another important part of the plan is to help those Nation members who want to start a business, operate an ongoing Nation business, or get training in a specific company. We provide training, advice, or opportunities to encourage these people.

My vision for the Nation is very positive. Enrolment in post-secondary education has risen from six students five years ago to more than thirty-five, and I see this continuing. I predict that more people will train in areas of community wellness and help turn negative things into positive things. Lifestyle patterns will change for the better.

I think people will go into business and do something for themselves and their families. I see a lot of family units pulling back together, including the larger families. It is very emotional to see the pride and excitement about progress in turning their lifestyles around.

This change means we will have a community that is close, where we are healed, where we can deal with our lives, where people can learn how to deal with their family lives and help each other.

Tsuu T'ina Nation is one of the leaders in terms of taking a Nation in a direction and reaching goals. We have many accomplishments that no other Nation has even considered doing. It gives me great pride to consider all of Tsuu T'ina Nation's achievements. It is overwhelming.

Experts from outside of the community often provide objective insights into the workings of the community. Trez McCaskill (1994, personal communication) has consulted with Tsuu T'ina Nation on management staffing issues for a number of years. His background is with the Department of Indian Affairs. He identifies strengths in the Nation:

They recognize the potential of their own members. For example, I feel very pleased to have been part of the recruitment of Darrell Crowchild. Darrell has untapped potential. Lack of formal training is offset by his grasp of the Nation's vision and his fifteen years experience working with the Nation. He has an appreciation of the government and other agencies, and he's very good with people. He handles the responsibilities that the Nation has given him. They have hired other key staff too. I offer a number of options and they choose the best option to address the situation they're dealing with.

Beyond the Nation members, I think that this community is well off, with many resources developed for their membership. They've taken whatever resources they have and managed them properly.

There are eleven businesses including reclamation, rental and lease of the land, Department of National Defence work, and the development of Redwood Meadows [golf course and housing development]. Nation members have an opportunity to advance and grow with these companies, which is really quite an accomplishment.

Jeanne Crowchild, a company general manager (1994, personal communication), is proud of the opportunities her children will have when they are adults:

We want to benefit our children. When they grow up, they're going to take over everything. They will see things differently, and I hope that they remember their roots, culture, and identity.

The future will be good if we work towards unity. My children are taught about the importance of unity. They see our family come together to discuss important issues in the community and to decide how we will vote together. They have seen how we can work with all people while still remembering our culture. This is what my father taught me.

Our national organization, Assembly of First Nations, has to communicate with communities across the country to build unity. Now all they do is argue. They forget our common goal. We can take the best things from each other and give the best things so we are strong as nations.

Carol Gottfriedson, a band member and a management consultant, has a long history of working in the band office. She too says that the work is for the children of the community (1994, personal communication) but acknowledges that things have not come easily to the community.

Nonetheless, I see us being just as competitive as the people across the road [mainstream society]. I think that they realize that now too. Our Nation has always had to work for what we have, and I think that's helped our success.

Our cultural perspective has also helped. A young person came to me. He confessed his concern that the old people say hard times are coming and we should be prepared. He said this talk frightens him. I shared the way it was explained to me. What we are doing now is preparing for those hard times. We will succeed and compete with the non-Indian population. We're preparing our children, and we're working towards something that they can have. They'll be able to look after themselves.

CODIFICATION OF
THE TSUU T'INA APPROACH

In 1985 the community reached a point where the leadership wanted to structure the operations of the Nation in a way that was understood by community members and by government and business interests. This included a board structure that is outlined in this and the next section.

Peter Manywounds (1994, personal conversation) describes the community's improving economic position: "Our cash flow has increased steadily from $5 million a year in the late seventies, to $15 million in 1990 to $45 million in 1994. Staff, chief and council, board members, and the community recognized the need to restructure to more effectively manage all projects. At our last count, we had 298 separate profit centres within the Nation."

Tsuu T'ina does not have an abundance of natural resources available for development. They have one gas well that generates a significant cash flow when industry prices are high. The cash generated through various projects was dramatically affected by the Finance Administration Act, passed in 1987 to increase stability. Many communities are concerned about the impact of a turnover in political leaders on administration matters. With the Finance Administration Act, decisions might take longer because of the learning curve, but it is useful in maintaining consistency.

This key document, Peter notes,

supports the whole operation and is central to the way banks understand the way we do business. Each department has a board of directors made up of community members and a councillor. Membership in the board of directors changes as some council members change. Council members are the shareholders of record and hold the assets in trust for all Nation citizens.

The overall direction and the corporate structure is secure because the Nation membership sees a record of success through financial benefits and jobs. Nation citizens vote changes to the act or to development plans. I don't believe that they would be prepared to make a wholesale change for political expediency. We've proven this structure and process works, to ourselves as well as to the outside business community. We would not jeopardize our current projects or walk away from our past achievements.

Further certainty was achieved when Nation citizens approved the Tsuu T'ina Heritage Trust Fund which divides Nation-owned company profits at year end. Peter describes the process:

For example, assume the ten companies generate a profit of $3.5 million. A formula process approved by the Nation dictates that I get 15 per cent off the top to operate my Economic Development program and carry out the economic development work that needs to be done on new start-ups.

Of the remaining 85 per cent, one-third is transferred to Nation citizens directly as a dividend payment. One-third is transferred to chief and council for their budget priorities. The final one-third is retained in the trust fund as our capital pool. Over a period of time, we have built that up to point where it becomes our equity – for example, in the multi-purpose building, the gas bar, or the golf course. The key to the process is that money is shared equally among the citizens chief and council, and the trust fund. It's always equitable and the balance stays in the fund. People get immediate benefits, but the Nation retains capital monies which can't be used for any other purpose except economic development. Dividends to community members have averaged from $700 to $1,000 per member.

The management structure is critical to the Nation's success.

MANAGING NATION BUSINESSES

Determining the role of the manager of a Nation business and the level of interaction with chief and council is a balance determined by a community's history. Tsuu T'ina Nation learned what worked for their community when Redwood Meadows, their first major project, faced difficulties. It required chief and council to handle political negotiations while the day-to-day operations were left to the manager and a small board. Peter Manywounds (1994, personal conversation) remembers:

Our leadership, management, and elders saw how well the structure worked. It was a good lesson for us and it's still evolving. Roles became clearer, so elected decision-makers have the final say, except in matters concerning land within the community. The whole community decides those matters.

With regards to budgets, council approves each item, line by line, so that they are familiar with all operations. They work with the treasury board that holds band capital and makes sure the budgets are properly set up and aligned for the whole Nation. Once those budgets are approved, then the chair of each board of directors works with the board and company management to make decisions such as the timing of expenditures, type of purchases, and timing of ongoing projects.

Council receives monthly financial statements, but they are not part of company day-to-day operations. Major budget changes are approved by council.

The treasury board is appointed by council with three commissioners and four council members. Its role is to manage the cash of the Nation and to monitor expenditures. It is a unique body performing a watchdog function. There is nothing like it across the country. One of the terms and conditions in the Finance Administration Act that affects the treasury board is that because it's the watchdog, four council members sit other than the four who have signing authority. They have no authority to spend money or to replace council's role.

Authorized spending limits for each level of operation are clearly set out in our Finance Administration Act. The board monitors operations, and if a manager is overspending, or something doesn't seem proper, they investigate. In the event that issue can't be resolved between the treasury board and the responsible board for that program, corporation, or economic development program, then it goes to council. It also advises chief and council on spending priorities.

You can appreciate that with ten companies, five or six economic development projects, and twenty or thirty departments, there is some fairly fierce competition for capital dollars. The treasury board ranks all capital requests based on priorities set by the Nation and then makes recommendations to council.

Relationships with off-reserve entities had begun to change years earlier. The move towards independence from the Department of Indian Affairs, for example, began in earnest in 1967. According to Peter, chief and council put their foot down and told Indian Affairs that they weren't needed all the time. If chief and council needed advice, then the department would be contacted. From that point, over twenty years ago, says Peter, "we have been making all the decisions here, albeit with advice from Indian Affairs or other people. We've made the decisions, and we've developed and grown. Over that period of time, chiefs, councils, and staff were wise enough to recognize that operations have to be constantly evaluated and re-evaluated."

After the Redwood Meadows experience, the board style of organization grew. It is unique to Tsuu T'ina Nation. Peter explains: "We have six boards that report directly to chief and council. We have a Department of National Defence to handle relations with the Canadian Forces base. We have the Nation Administration Board which handles all of the Nation-funded programs: housing, membership, roads, lands, and all service delivery. The Inter-governmental Affairs Board handles all government-funded programs: social services, education, health care, Spirit Healing Lodge, and a number of others."

Development projects are incubated in the Economic Development department and fall under the purview of the Economic Development Board, an independent entity. Once a company is determined to be self-sufficient and fully operational, then a formal transfer of responsibility is made from the Economic Development Board to the Companies Board. Peter works with two boards, "the Economic Development Board, which is responsible for all economic development in the community, and the Companies Board, which is actually the operating board for all of our corporations."

The relationship between the Economic Development and Companies boards is close, says Peter. "For example, the commercial centre is now a viable operating entity that was started under the guidance of the Economic Development Board. A week and half ago the boards met, and we did a formal transfer by resolution, and authority was passed from the Economic Development Board to the Companies Board ... It is a significant project worth over $2,000,000 a year in cash flow."

Generally, two council members are appointed by the chief to each board, and three citizens at large are also appointed by the chief and council. People with a background or interest in economic development will likely be asked to sit on that board. "With a small community like ours," says Peter, "everybody knows everybody else, and knows their background. It's not that difficult to be reasonable about who is selected. We have various advisors who sit on our boards who may not be band citizens."

TRAINING AND EMPLOYMENT

The goal set by chief and council is to train and employ band citizens for all positions within the Nation. Economic development initiatives and band companies focus on training whenever and wherever possible.

From Peter's perspective, the philosophy of the Nation is to maintain control, and this is demonstrated by the fact that Nation citizens hold most of the senior administration positions.

Some of the finance and accounting positions are held by non-citizens, but everyone else including the general managers are band citizens. Some former managers didn't understand and came in thinking they could do almost as they chose because they knew best. We ran into real problems with some bad decisions that were out of our control. As a result we made a commitment that we weren't going to do that kind of thing again.

We do partner with advisors and companies who share their expertise. We've got advisory staff in education, a company that acts as an advisor on our construction projects, and our agricultural joint venture makes room for farmers who have farmed here for years. The list goes on.

Human resource development, however, was recognized as a priority early on. Chief and council emphasize the effort needed in training our citizens on the job or in special training courses. Our upgrading program had sixty students in 1993 and twenty-eight graduates with Grade 12 equivalency in April. In less than a year we delivered people with training. Twenty-eight people were subsequently employed in the band structure or continued to post-secondary education.

INSIGHTS FOR SUCCESS

Chief Whitney is clear about his community's needs. When he deals with a bank that does not share the community vision, he is cautious. He explains:

Development proposals that are accepted by the community fit the needs of our community. Conventional knowledge in the greater society may not agree with our wisdom and knowledge. The banking industry may react to a proposal by saying tough economic times mean we're leery of this type of development and it won't succeed. I say, where are we going to go? We'll always be here. We're not going to create an industry, a company, or a business that isn't going to survive for our people. They turn us down just because it doesn't fit into their conventional knowledge of development.

What we've had to do is take a two-tier perspective. We identified conventional knowledge for bankers and funders. We also know the wisdom of aboriginal people in this community. We develop two packages of information with one meeting the needs of our community and the other for bankers. It brings the balance of their way of thinking and melds it with ours without affecting how we do our business within our own community.

Chief Whitney says the big difference between the two approaches is that the community puts people first. Education or employment opportunities with cultural and traditional values carry great weight in determining opportunities for the community. Profitability is important, but it is not the determining factor in choosing suitable projects. "If a project is not financially viable, then it doesn't meet the needs and human values of our people in providing bread and butter for their children," Chief Whitney explains. "While it is not first priority, it is a factor we consider in developing our economic needs. We want to be financially secure and successful. For example, the multi-purpose complex needed projects that ensured the retail and commercial aspects of the building were secured so that the building would become viable. Once we secured proper leases, then we were able to go into our community and say that it is financially secure and we have that safety net. Next we incorporate our people into that safety net to ensure that we meet the needs of this generation and the next seven generations."

Community communication and decision-making processes are critical as the future of the community is determined. Peter Manywounds describes Tsuu T'ina Nation's approach:

Chief and council hold two-day Nation member meetings semi-annually where they talk about all the business in the community. Staff present reports and discuss all the current and planned projects. Motions are made by the citizens from the floor that issue directives to council on particular matters.

Once a year we hold shareholders meetings where each company or program sets up a booth that is staffed by management or employees. Any Nation member can come in and get specific information. It is not a big meeting where people might be too intimidated to ask questions. They may ask for specific details about economic development projects, Nation companies, or future plans or get information about getting involved through training or education.

They note any concerns on suggestion sheets. Suggestions are compiled and directed to the appropriate board. They may be good ideas for making things better or increasing benefits for citizens. These suggestions are usually implemented by the board. Alternatively, if it's an idea that has merit but is beyond the scope of a particular board, it would go to chief and council for further action at council's discretion.

Our doors are always open to shareholders. We've got nothing to hide from our public. That's a difference that we sometimes have to point out to non-Nation citizens. It is Nation business, and Nation members have the opportunity to look at the plans or the books any time. We don't make that offer to the general public.

While the communication process has been given a lot of thought, chief and council review it regularly and suggest improvements. The reviews result in directives to improve communication with Nation members. "Members need to get answers, but the sheer volume of reports on these operations is staggering for council members to assimilate and explain projects in detail," Peter comments. "We work with these projects every day so we can help by providing complete information to Nation members."

PROJECT GENESIS AND DEVELOPMENT

Tsuu T'ina Nation has developed a process of evaluating projects with the guidance of chief and council and the assistance of staff and Nation citizens. The process has been influenced by hard lessons and history.

Many unsolicited projects are submitted to Tsuu T'ina Nation, and project ideas are also generated by staff and by chief and council. These ideas are vetted by the Economic Development department through a strenuous screening process that determines their feasibility.

All members are given the opportunity for input into projects. The Elders Committee give advice and feedback, once a project is determined to be feasible. The community also has the opportunity to give direction on projects since projects may still be cancelled although they were labelled as feasible by the Economic Development department.

Feasible projects are then brought to chief and council. Chief Whitney, describes the consultation process: "We start off with the council and elders. I seek input personally to be sure that our planning has strength and wisdom. We carry the knowledge of the old into the new. Their guidance forms the root to a new tree that we are working on with each project. Then we involve the young people in the building of that tree."

Darrell Crowchild oversees the Elders program that keeps all elders informed and gives them the opportunity to contribute to Nation business. He has strong personal feelings for the program: "I have been very, very fortunate to take care of the Elders program," he says. Few people have such a chance to get to know the elders. I am privileged to understand their concerns, to listen and talk to them and know how important they are in our lives and within our Nation. We meet once or twice a month, and I arrange for consultants to help explain technical language so they know exactly what is going on within the Nation. Program and company managers come in and speak to the elders too."

Carol Gottfriedson notes that land is a critical part of the feasibility analysis. "We look at land issues that have to be dealt with, including designation of the land. In some projects that part of the process can take almost two years. It has to go through votes in our membership and through community workshops. Nation citizens are fully aware of project plans now and in the future. This process includes everyone and is one of the strengths of Tsuu T'ina Nation."

An outline of the screening approach used in the Economic Development department provides insight into a thorough screening strategy. It begins when a business proposition is made to the Nation such as an offer to lease, or a joint venture opportunity. The first question asked is: Do we want to consider the proposal?

An initial screening process begins, involving the general manager of economic development, the project officer trainee, and one of the finance people. If it is a $250,000 project, for example, then in-house staff evaluate it. If it is a $5 million project, then external consulting advice is sought. Ninety per cent of unsolicited proposals are screened out. Reasons include that it's not feasible; it doesn't fit with Nation plans; or it's not a suitable use of funds that would receive approval.

Business plans may be financially feasible, with good rates of return, good management, and financing, and still be screened out. For example, a welding operation looked impressive, but it did not meet the community's by-law requirements regarding environmental concerns.

Additional steps may include passing a borderline proposal to finance and economic development managers. If a proposal has passed

initial screening, however, then more information is sought. A comprehensive business plan including information on management, products/
services, financing, and cash-flow projections must be submitted. This
information is necessary to move the proposal along and also demonstrates the seriousness of the applicant. Confidentiality restrictions are
in effect so the information is secure. The finance and economic development managers review the new information. Further screening occurs. For example, joint venture proposals must be structured in favour
of +50.1 per cent band ownership in the business so the community
maintains operational control.

Proposals are then submitted to the chief for review by council, the
Elders Committee, and the community.

NATION PROJECT INVESTMENTS

Nation projects currently in operation vary in size, industry, and location. Peter describes some of them:

Redwood Meadows golf course has the longest profit history. Redwood Meadows, a land development project, has shown a profit since 1988. These profits
were delayed because of a number of problems including marketing and regula-
tory problems.

The gravel operation, which is not on designated land, has been very profitable. It's the closest pit in this quadrant of the city, and although the quality of
material is not number one, our location, access, and competitive pricing make
it very marketable.

The Wolf Flat Ordinance Disposal Corporation clears land of leftover explo-
sives so that the land is reusable. There are not very many people in this field.
Our advantages were that we own the land and have strong corporate capability.
We hope the land will be reclaimed in 1997–98, but we continually discover that
the project is bigger than first realized. In any event, the very involved process is
repeated three or four times, leaving a minuscule chance that an explosive is
missed. The lease with the military runs until the year 2005. Getting the land
cleared is part of the process of regaining use of that land. We will farm it once it
is reuseable. Its proximity and location to the city makes it is a very valuable
piece of property. One possibility, if we decide to develop, is a new ski hill that
would have the longest run near the city. It would be twice or three times as long
as Canada Olympic Park and twice as long as Wintergreen, two local ski hills.

We're in the process of trying to expand that company to bid on and secure
contracts in other parts of the world. Our goal is to operate a year-round com-

pany with contracts in climates where we can work over the winter months and spend the summer period here.

THE SCREENING PROCESS

The process for prioritizing development objectives and screening projects has developed over a long period. Outside consultants supported a community process of creating master development plans that build on unique opportunities existing due to proximity to the city of Calgary. A thorough screening process identifies opportunities worthy of pursuit. It has been a tough experience to get to this point, Peter recalls:

There were some fundamental changes in philosophy and attitude that began many years ago that led us to where we are today. The first change occurred when I was young and not directly involved. We would make decisions knowing that we were going to make mistakes, but we'd make the mistakes ourselves and learn from them. That was a very fundamental choice that the community took in the late sixties and early seventies.

The second important decision was fundamental. Instead of trying to create employment as the main goal, which is what the government have been trying to sell, a conscious decision was taken in 1980 that we weren't going to try to create jobs for the sake of employment. We were going to create businesses for profit. If we couldn't create a business that was going to make a profit, we weren't going to do it, because we believe – and I think we've since proven – if we create a business that makes a profit, we create stable long-term employment for citizens.

We had tough experiences with the Redwood Meadows housing and golf course project. It taught us that we could meet problems with banks and legislation that were costly if we persisted. Steve Runner was the band manager in 1982, and he felt that there was a real need to divide economic development activities from band management and delivery of programs and services. That change was accepted, and we operated that way for about eight years. It gave us time and the impetus for planning and development. We thoroughly examined different projects without being controversial about it.

Many solicited and unsolicited business proposals are submitted for consideration by the community. Without a community vision for the future of Tsuu T'ina and a process to evaluate submissions, it would be difficult to know what projects should be developed. Projects in 1994 included a magnificent multi-purpose building, with another golf course on the drawing board and a business park to be built on a strip of land bordering the community boundary.

According to Peter, six to eight proposals a week are received from all kinds of people, with more than one hundred annually going through a thorough screening process. Few of the one hundred proposals make it through to the end, Peter says. "We don't have to jump at the first deal that's offered to us, the one that may look great on the face of it. So we go through this process that we have put on a chart and taken a lot of time to develop. We also work on our own [projects] including a hotel and a twin arena complex. It's in those first four steps where 99 per cent of the proposals are screened out as being unsuitable. We then reach a decision point as to whether or not we continue the process. Quite frankly, we don't want to waste time on a project that is not going to work."

The screening process was developed collaboratively between Tsuu T'ina staff and their auditors. This joint effort formalized the informal processes already followed by the Economic Development staff. The well-honed screening process now results in well-planned five-year projections for each Nation company, giving better control over human and financial resources.

Peter gives more detail: the five year plans are reviewed and updated annually for each company, he says. "The Economic Development department oversees several approved projects. Time-lines for the Buffalo Run golf course indicate that we'll start construction in the spring, and we're scheduled to be fully operational by the spring of 1996. Those things are all charted out on bar graphs and include time frames, decision points, and responsibilities. Charts show the schedule, where problems may have cropped up, and what's been done. There is no way that you can manage large projects without these tools."

In his opinion, "probably the most significant difference I find compared to a lot of other tribes" is that "the chief and council made decisions and set policies that allow us to get on with the work without political interference."

Difficult issues can arise where politics and business collide and are the undoing of many projects in many communities. The original housing and golf course project called Redwood Meadows provided some difficult learning opportunities, Peter recalls.

We had experiences with Redwood Meadows that tested our policy at that time, which was "We'll make the decisions and learn from our mistakes." We learned that chief and council can't micro-manage business because their motivation is political. To try to apply that motivation in a business world doesn't work. We have tried mixing politics and business, and we've proven through some fairly major mistakes that it's going to cost us money.

There are problems, but the system works. Sometimes it frustrates the politicians because they feel they are not being listened to, but on the other hand it has been proven that the system works. We are making money, and so while there are problems, politics don't enter into the day-to-day operations. Council issues the directives, and we implement them. As long as we successfully carry out the directives issued by council, politics is left out of the business side of the Nation.

Other safeguards exist to protect community interests. For example, chief and council are bound by the limits outlined in the process of deciding uses for designated lands. According to the Indian Act, Nation members vote on a proposal through a referendum process. They agree to designate the land for specific purposes. For example, the business park, the golf course, the multi-purpose building, and the commercial centre are specifically designated through this process. Neither the Nation nor the government nor anybody else can undertake other projects beyond the scope set out in the referendum. At the end of seventy-five years, all interests revert back to the Nation. Peter observes, "We don't carry financing on these projects for longer than twenty or twenty-five years anyway, so lending institutions are paid out well before the expiration of the seventy-five designation term."

Projects must also conform to the community land-use by-law which is administered by the Planning Commission. It is a very detailed guideline approved by the community and provides details on a variety of issues covering development on designated land. Peter elaborates:

Our by-law covers the same things as any municipal land use or zoning bylaw and includes such things as the height of structures, setbacks from roads, architectural controls and guidelines, signage, handling waste, and restricting development to be compatible with the area. It is sanctioned by chief and council so it's got some teeth. A group of community members and consultants make up the Planning Commission that is separate from the Economic Development and Company boards, to minimize any chance of conflict of interest.

We're set up to monitor the interests of the Nation, but we each have a little different point of view. Our by-law is very complete and encompasses everything you can imagine. Other community bylaws that I'm aware of might deal with the issues that are specifically pertinent to what they're doing now. We wanted a body to control all development, make applications, and deal with permits, and our membership would best be served doing it this way.

Once a project is submitted for review, it usually takes the zoning committee four to six weeks to review it. In the event of a dispute involving the Planning Commission, it goes to chief and council to be resolved. It is an internal process, but it part of the checks and balances. We want to make sure we're doing things in the most beneficial way for the community.

We've learned collectively that good business and management skills by themselves aren't enough for this kind of a setting. Politics and sensitivity to community members are always required. This is a small community. You must understand that a member employee may require discipline, suspension, or dismissal as may happen with any company. Otherwise you can't operate efficiently and make a profit.

On the other side of it, you have to deal with sensitivity because, hey, we all live here, and we're not going anywhere. In the city you fire someone if the job isn't done properly, and you never see them again. Here, you may let a person go, but they have to understand what happened. If they made a mistake, then we try to help them correct it, with the emphasis on helping people to be successful. In this size of an operation there's just no way that you can expect everybody to perform 100 per cent.

Orientation of employees is critical to the success of our operations. They need to know going in what we expect from them, whether it's a gas jockey, a chartered accountant, or an engineer. They receive half or a full day with their supervisor so they understand the operation, where they fit in, and what's expected of them. New employees are closely supervised for a period of two weeks or a month, to make sure that they are comfortable with things. They also receive help with personal problems or whatever kinds of things that may pop up, to try and help them be successful.

That's the theory, and I'm not saying that every person is on board. In almost two years that I've been here now, I've found that everybody is eager to help because they understand and are comfortable with where we are going. They see the fantastic opportunities we have – although our younger people need to be more involved in making successful careers for themselves.

OUR STRENGTH IS OUR PEOPLE

Darrell reflects on the place of culture in Tsuu T'ina Nation:

We have faith in our young people and we keep our elders involved. Our culture is always with us, and we often don't realize it. It's in the way we have a meeting, or the way we meet with people, and the way we approach the issues. We are trying to bring back our language, and regularly we seek guidance from our spiritual leaders. We begin our council meetings with prayer. We always give thanks to the Creator for all the gifts he has given us, for the life he has given to our people, for helping us throughout tough times, for giving us the strength to go on and go beyond. And we give thanks for the elders we can rely on for advice, guidance, and the language. Our family is also our strength. We are all related, and our strength just builds and builds and builds. We still have a lot of work to do to address social problems, but there are a lot of positive things about us.

Family is very important to many Nation citizens. Jeanne Crowchild, company manager, reflects on the important roles of family members in the community.

As a woman and a mother, I tell my daughter to remember who she is and that she will have to work harder than her brother will but she can do it. I have role models who are women, like my mother. They are very strong, independent people. My father and my grandfather are my role models and give me another way of looking at things. If I'm unsure of one person's advice, I'll go to another person for advice. I'll think about both perspectives and then I'll act, based on a combination of the advice.

Elder Helen Maguiness shares her thoughts on the importance of land to Nation elders and to the community:

The community asks us to go to them, and sometimes we don't like what they are doing. We are very scared for our land. The land is very sacred to us. We don't want to even let go of five acres. I don't even know how big five acres is, but we are very stingy. There are a lot of young people that will be eighteen or nineteen, and when they want to get married, they have to build a house.

We think that we are running out of land and it is getting crowded. We are thinking of the future for our grandchildren and their children. We want them to always have the land. If they sell it, our land will be gone and the money will be gone. We have got nothing. So we try to tell our young people that: "Don't let the money fool you, because we don't have much land." We got pretty country here. There is snow on the mountains in the winter too, the mountain there has snow on it, and it is pretty.

Hal Eagletail, a young adult and Economic Development staff member, talks further about the land and the Nation's development philosophy.

While tourism is another Nation focus, public access to Tsuu T'ina territory is carefully monitored:

We tell people that we're open for business, and we mean it. With regards to our business park, we're only open for business up to the quarter-mile line. We're inviting people into our territory into the business park, but not to go west.

Our tourism project is another good example of how we restrict access to our territory. Access is very controlled. Bus tours only go to designated locations, and they're always accompanied by a tour guide who is a Nation member ... The bottom-line philosophy is we're going to take advantage of what's available to us for economic development, but we're going to preserve about 98 per cent of the reserve for the community for the members to enjoy as they choose, without interference from the outside. This philosophy is very key to our members being comfortable with what we're doing.

WOMEN'S CONTRIBUTIONS

Women are acknowledged as a strength in the community. They offer strong support and leadership in the family and community, as well as guidance for the young people. With this important resource comes advice from women who are in positions of authority.

Delphine Pipestem, the director of the Adult Learning Centre, is currently a graduate student in the Environmental Design program at the University of Calgary. Her first degree is in political studies and management. Delphine maintains that women are "our biggest strength in the community":

Although there are no women on council now, there have been in the past. The majority of management positions are held by women, and it is the women who recognize the need for more formal training and are going to school to further their education, as indicated in the post-secondary and upgrading statistics. They are willing to enhance their skills and take on the challenge. I feel this is due to the inherent strength of native women. They hold the community together because they hold the family together. They value the community as they value their family. There are a lot of social problems in our community, and it is the women who have the strength and the courage to bring these issues to light. The healing of our community is slowly being integrated into the overall community development process, and it is usually the women who are most involved in the healing process.

The programs started by Tsuu T'ina women which Delphine feels best demonstrate their strength include a wellness program, a program to deal with child apprehension, and counselling-skill training program for educators. In particular, the wellness program came out of a desire by a group of women to address community social problems, including the drug use and high suicide rates among their young people. Another group of women spearheaded the Early Prevention program in order to work with families and avoid child apprehension. Finally, all education staff received counselling training to help children in Nation schools.

While economic development concentrates on profits and employment, these women have focused on the healing that is necessary for a successful journey to self-reliance and self-sufficiency. These programs help members feel good about themselves and so complete the circle.

Other band citizens express similar sentiments regarding the strength of women in Tsuu T'ina society. Hal Eagletail sees women as the "secret to the healing" of every First Nation.

If women were to create a society amongst themselves that would address the concerns of economic development or cultural preservation, there would be unbelievable power to effect change. I believe in our culture the women's role has always been important. The way I was taught is that woman was given the opportunity to bring life into the world, and man was given the opportunity to make song with the drum. The song reflects all human emotions whether it be happiness, sadness, jealousy or fearfulness.

There are many critical areas in living where the woman and the man maintain a balance of input into decisions which our leaders must remember. Women are strong and tend to operate most community wellness programs, but it is important that there be balance and that men become more involved in our community's health.

Carol Gottfriedson recalls the advice her father gave her when she assumed her position as administrator in the band office: "It's hard to be accepted in different positions as a woman, and so I went to my father. He told me to be very careful in making decisions. The young people are capable of looking after themselves, and remember any decisions will affect the little ones. Make sure that they can carry out your decisions and that they do not hinder the little ones in any way."

SUMMARY

Tsuu T'ina Nation's story of success is of a community that has chosen to follow its own path. While that path has included obstacles, it has not been dictated to the Nation by outsiders, and its lessons have been taken to heart by its leaders.

Tsuu T'ina Nation is living its vision for a healthy, strong community, on its own terms. Yet Tsuu T'ina remains a quiet success story. Hal Eagletail explains why. "We don't want to be held up as an example for other First Nations. Once that happens, there is the risk that other communities are not encouraged to follow their own path," he says.

"Our path is not a guarantee of success for others. Each community must develop their own direction that capitalizes on local opportunities. We share our success with those who come to visit our community rather than put our stories in the media. I am proud of our philosophy of good business since we are trying to balance our cultural distinctness with economic growth."

3

Winnipeg's Aboriginal Community

WINNIPEG'S ABORIGINAL COMMUNITY, MANITOBA, demonstrates a vitality and commitment that has resulted in a strong community presence. The Aboriginal Centre is the hub and is owned by community organizations. Many service organizations are housed there, while many others operate throughout the core area and beyond. First Nations and Métis people are well represented with specific political organizations dedicated to their needs as well as by an organization that looks at the needs of all urban Aboriginal people. Partnerships are evident and support services for all types of economic development initiatives are available. Making "community" meaningful in a setting that is usually anonymous is a daunting task, but the results mirror Winnipeg's diverse population.

For the estimated 50 to 70 per cent of the Aboriginal community residing in villages, towns, and cities throughout the country, important questions endure. How can a population with a shared heritage develop with strength? How can these urban Aboriginal peoples meet the same dreams for self-sufficiency as their brothers and sisters on reserve or in settlements? Can the challenges of poor education, poverty, and lack of opportunity be overcome in a large, anonymous city?

The power of economic development in an urban setting is only part of the solution. Many services are in place to support the urban Aboriginal population including community and government sponsored organizations in social services, employment, and education. Winnipeg, which in 1991 and 1996 had the largest urban Aboriginal population of all major Canadian cities, is a reasonable place to examine these issues facing urban Aboriginal communities across the country.

Winnipeg has many Aboriginal organizations that were established to meet the needs of the Aboriginal community in adapting to urban life. According to the Social Planning Council of Winnipeg in a 1998 internal report on Population and Labour Force Dynamics, by 2001 Aboriginal peoples were expected to make up 15 per cent of the provincial population and 10.4 per cent of the city of Winnipeg (or 73, 800). Aboriginal unemployment was three times that of the rate for the general population, or 21 per cent. Aboriginal youth unemployment for those 15–24 years of age was twice the rate of all city youth, or 28.9 per cent. While over half of Aboriginal women participated in the workforce in 1991, unemployment rates for this segment remained at twice the overall female rate, or 18 per cent. Aboriginal adults were projected to represent 9–10 per cent of the Winnipeg labour force in 2001.

These projections point to large challenges and opportunities facing the country. Aboriginal peoples will impact the country positively as their potential is developed. They will be a drain on resources if social and economic issues are not dealt with effectively. What approaches are being taken by the Aboriginal community in Winnipeg as they move to make positive differences?* Who are some of the leaders and what strategies are being used? But, first of all, what is the vision of and for the community?

The Winnipeg scene is vibrant and unique. It has been the subject of work by economist John Loxley (1994, 2000) suggesting what is successful and strategies for building on its strengths. The province worked with the Aboriginal community to develop the Urban Aboriginal Strategy. Key participants George Campbell and Brett Eckstein share some insights into an interesting process. The Aboriginal Centre was conceived of by the directors of a number of non-profit Aboriginal organizations, who brought people and Aboriginal organizations to a single location in an inner city district with a high Aboriginal population. Wayne Helgason and Bill Shead share their project start-up memories and assess its current status. Part of the vision for the centre was an Aboriginal business centre. Sean Kocsis and Len Flett are integral to the success of the Aboriginal Business Development Centre and share their insights.

* A number of significant local and provincial groups are making a difference. Only a few were selected for this study, in order to set the context for some significant projects. Some groups including the Assembly of Manitoba Chiefs, the Manitoba Métis Federation, and the Canadian Council for Aboriginal Business are doing significant work in this area but are not included here due to resource and time constraints.

The political element is less clear regarding urban-based Aboriginal peoples. Historically, status Indians living off reserve have had their legal ties to benefits broken. In that vacuum the Aboriginal Council of Winnipeg was formed to meet the needs of Aboriginal peoples in Winnipeg. Over time its mandate has become less clear, and program dollars may be available to Manitoba Métis Federation and the Assembly of Manitoba Chiefs as their communities move to accept responsibility for the needs of all their members, no matter where they reside. This puts three organizations in direct competition for dollars and urban-based constituency. The inevitable conflict is evident. Mary Richard, Sean Koscis, and George Munroe comment on the Aboriginal Council.

Youth are an important part of the process, and their organization of Aboriginal Youth With Initiative, Inc. is described by Lawrence Angeconeb, Heather Milton, and Clay Thomas Müeller. AYWI have plans for more active youth in the decision-making process and making a real difference through needed projects. They have a unique structure and interesting projects on the go.

Understanding diversity and how to make room for everyone's vision is important in comprehending Winnipeg's experience. It is dynamic, with the usual energetic discussion about the best way to accomplish goals. The projects and programs examined in the following sections will give the reader some sense of the breadth of experience that is Winnipeg's Aboriginal scene.

THE PEOPLE SPEAK:
URBAN ABORIGINAL STRATEGY

Federal and provincial governments are redefining their obligations to Aboriginal peoples as the urbanization trend continues. The costs of services to Aboriginal peoples are steep as each tries to determine a "fair" distribution of this obligation. However, effective policy does not stop at the obvious jurisdictional questions between governments. Instead it moves past to ask how these needs can be met effectively and creatively, with room for all those people who want to contribute to solutions.

The Manitoba Roundtable for the Environment and the Economy, made up of individuals from the community and government, was established from 1989 through to 1999 to review all sustainable development policies. According to Brett Eckstein, the senior analyst for the

Sustainable Development unit, the roundtable process has many advantages that make it attractive and has been explored by other jurisdictions including the Clinton administration in the United States. Individuals sit as individuals and not as representatives of their organizations. This allows for more freedom of discussion since members are not binding their organizations with their comments and can thoroughly canvas ideas under discussion.

Brett (personal communication, 1997) describes some of the Manitoba Roundtable's unique features:

It is at arm's length from the government but as much as the roundtable is a creation of government and has seven cabinet members on it, the discussions are amazing, in an open and relaxed atmosphere. The premier openly disagrees with cabinet ministers and members of the roundtable. Cabinet ministers and members of the roundtable disagree with the premier. It is a real healthy atmosphere for discussing larger issues. There is a lot of consensus among participants who represent diverse groups such as labour, business, environment, Aboriginal peoples, and consumers.

There is a close working relationship with government with cabinet ministers being part of the consensus process. Understanding and support may build for an otherwise challenged document. The prior discussion helps in improving support that might not be generated if the government is left out of the consultation process. The grassroots consultation has to occur at the same time. This holistic approach makes the roundtable process a test bed for new policy issues and promotes a process which is not bogged down in political baggage. Roundtable and grassroots issues that are discussed in this think tank become familiar to cabinet members who have increased sensitivity, and thus there are benefits for all parties involved.

An Aboriginal advisory committee was struck in 1996 as part of the roundtable strategy to develop a strategy for Aboriginal peoples. George Campbell was named chair of the committee and brought to bear a wealth of knowledge and experience of his community. He suggested that the roundtable examine Aboriginal issues affecting the sustainability of the community. While the issues may be relevant to other parts of the province, a decision was taken to restrict the strategy to Winnipeg.

George noticed an unchanging disparity between Aboriginal peoples who were employed and had decent housing and those who suffered in poverty. He recalls (personal communication, 1998):

I was very concerned with what was negative. It is our people that come to Winnipeg to find their place and try to start a new life. They found difficulty in their home communities and didn't fit into this society in Winnipeg. Seeing our people fall by the wayside made it impossible to ignore. I suggested we review what was going on and what things might or could be changed that would benefit our people. A committee was formed to develop an urban Aboriginal strategy with a group of Aboriginal members to act as an advisory council.

I think this council was important, as were our forums with grassroots people. Youth were targeted since they are the future of our community. We held workshops in the area where our Aboriginal peoples live. We had six workshops with well over a thousand people attending. Great work resulted from these workshops by the participants themselves. Mostly Aboriginal peoples attended with a good representation of non-Aboriginal peoples too. We have to work together, and our final report picks up the essence of what the grassroots people were telling us. There is nothing new or startling, but it is a comprehensive strategy that brings the report findings of education, housing, safety, and economic development into focus.

While the federal and provincial governments decided who must meet the needs of the urban Aboriginal community, the Manitoba provincial government acknowledged the necessity of going beyond the current ineffective institutional processes to re-examine delivery of services. Development of the urban Aboriginal strategy through the roundtable process was an opportunity to build capacity and move forward with a broad base of discussion and input, according to Wayne Helgason, the executive director of the Social Planning Council of Winnipeg. Moreover, it spoke to building a strong, sustainable community. As Wayne (personal communication, 1997) notes, "Aboriginal peoples want a pleasurable life style like everyone and the freedom to be Aboriginal in the way they want, including practising cultural beliefs and associating with who they want and in the manner they want. I don't think it means being absorbed into the mainstream society, but I think it means being involved and setting their own definitions and boundaries on their terms."

BUILDING AN URBAN ABORIGINAL STRATEGY

The process of building an urban Aboriginal strategy remained apolitical while jurisdictional issues remained unresolved. Support for the initiative was garnered from various departments in the provincial government as well from the city of Winnipeg and the federal government. Statistics formed the basis of the early discussions, Brett Eckstein recalls. The focus was on trying to understand what these statistics meant to the community:

We didn't want to start with issues so we looked at some of the statistics as the basis for our discussion paper. It was hard putting some statistics down on paper. For example, six out of ten non-Aboriginal peoples own homes. Only two out ten Aboriginal peoples own homes. What does that mean when you realize 43 per cent of Aboriginal peoples live in the core area? Where do the others live? They are living in the suburbs that are supposed to be more affluent, but there are affluent people living in the core area too. So what does that tell?

The statistics around single parents indicate that primarily single mothers tend to live in the core area. That is where people say the problems are. You must remember housing is cheaper in the core area so that is why you would tend to live there. It makes sense because if you look at immigration of other groups, where do people go when they move to the city of Winnipeg? Generally into the core areas or cheaper housing if they are poor.

My grandmother moved to Winnipeg as a single mother and found a room in an attic in the core area. You know it was cheap. I think that little has changed, and some reasons underlying the statistics are no different than for other people.

A workshop series was held in which grassroots people joined other participants to discuss a process that built commitment to the results through involvement. The large group of two hundred or three hundred people was divided into groups around the issues. They worked together to develop a presentation to the plenary session. Dinner was shared and then presentations were made. The feedback formed the basis of a draft report that was discussed at the next workshop. George enjoyed seeing younger people step in as facilitators in various discussion groups.

Comments and feedback were collected and a final strategy recommended. Brett then compiled the information in the draft report. He comments on the process:

We did very well. We spent $40,000, which is very reasonable for the amount of people who participated. We had over a thousand people attend six meetings. We tried to create categories for issues that roughly followed the categories for sustainable development. It formed an holistic framework for completing draft documents.

The government-policy people wanted something that could be implemented, so while there was focus on getting feedback on the drafts, there was also focus on an action plan. Objectives were identified for each target. We looked for a time-frame with benchmarks for where we are today that could help us in setting reasonable objectives. For example, questions were asked about statistics for single parents in the core area. If that changes, do we solve all of the problems?

There are problems in the suburbs that are very similar to what goes on in the core, but they really are not concentrated, or you see them and you don't hear about them. How do they fit in?

Implementation of the plan had to be discussed including who had responsibility as well as details about monitoring, evaluation, and reporting. What is the mechanism for actually getting this stuff done? This was important because I would say that the number-one problem is cynicism when dealing with government, in the Aboriginal community. They have been consulted and consulted, and nothing changes.

The Aboriginal Advisory Council was integral to this process. The members were involved from the beginning and were called on whenever possible to provide guidance to the roundtable sub-committee. The main goal was to get the process moving forward and maintain the momentum once the final report was published. This is a unique process that has not been undertaken in other urban centres.

George Campbell notes that some essential factors must be in place to make the process successful:

I think first of all, the community, in this case the Aboriginal community, had to want to participate in something like this. That is why we had to do a lot of work to introduce the idea up front. People had to understand what was going to happen in the process. Once we got the message out in various ways, people showed up because they were interested in being a part of this unique idea of participating in developing strategy.

This strategy is their own. They can claim ownership of it. Government authorities allowed this to be an apolitical process. It was great to be able to publish a document that was really from the grassroots, speaking to those in authority. I think that we were successful in accomplishing our objectives. We kept it status blind so that we wanted to hear from anyone who is Aboriginal. We didn't break our discussion groups into groups according to status – First Nations, Métis, and Inuit. That was a plus.

The implementation of the final recommendations focuses on the responsibility of all groups in society including individuals, families,

communities, corporations, and the various levels of government. It will
not succeed otherwise. This consultation, in Brett's opinion, would be
one of the most successful of the roundtable consultations. A policy application document was released on 7 July 1999, and memorandum of
understanding was signed by the provincial and federal governments.

Some expected that the community would whine about problems
and demand money be committed for more programs. This did not
happen. It became obvious that there are gaps in services that require
an investment, but the overwhelming feeling was that the participants
wanted to be part of the strategy and make a difference. They want to
be treated as equals with something of value to say. They are living the
problems, and the solutions are important to them. The connection to
the grassroots is critical, and the need to bring partners to the table in
order to make significant change is essential, according to George.

The final recommendations follow along with other studies. A focus on
environmental concerns is woven throughout the recommendations that
relate to poverty, low levels of education, housing, safety issues, employment, and economic development. The difference with this work is that
the grassroots can buy into a strategy that they helped form, and the Sustainable Development unit, through Brett's work, informs those in senior
levels of government about the urban Aboriginal strategy. The unit has
some freedom that allows creativity and effectiveness to thrive in its work.

While the Aboriginal Advisory Council disbanded upon completion
of the final report, the Aboriginal Council of Winnipeg has agreed to
help monitor the progress of implementation. Other organizations will
also ensure that the recommendations are properly executed. This partnership will continue.

The urban Aboriginal strategy workshops were held at the Aboriginal
Centre, in the heart of the North End. This area is home to many Aboriginal peoples, and the centre is one of the projects that is helping to
build a cohesive Aboriginal community in an urban setting.

GATHERING COMMUNITY:
THE ABORIGINAL CENTRE OF WINNIPEG

In the 1970s, Aboriginal community leaders conceived of a plan that
would bring services for Aboriginal peoples together in the Neeginan
(Our Place) project. It took until the late 1980s to take the project
from a dream to reality. In 1988 the directors of several large non-

profit organizations providing services to Winnipeg's Aboriginal population began talking about ways to replace high rental costs with more reasonable lease expenses in their own building. It made sense, and a study suggested they could either purchase an existing building or build a new one. Canadian Pacific Railroad had a station for sale in a central location.

The significance of the CP building reached beyond the Aboriginal community to new Canadians and to those with an appreciation for architecture. "The building has enormous historical importance to Manitobans because it is the site where many immigrants came by rail through the CP railway station," notes Bill Shead, former chief executive officer (personal communication, 1998). "Many soldiers, sailors and airmen left from this railway station to go overseas in World War I, World War II and the Korean War. There were others who simply got the train to Winnipeg Beach or took it across country. There are a lot of memories within the building. From an architectural standpoint, it has real importance, as it is one of the few architectural examples of the Maxwell brothers' work in Winnipeg and perhaps in all of Canada ... it was designated a heritage site."

Wayne Helgason was at that time the director of Mamawi Wichi Itata Centre, a family social service agency, and was involved in early discussions. He reminisces about the process:

We had to be seen to be more than deliverers of service. We had to articulate a vision and work towards a vision, of having much greater impact with the little resources that we had. As Aboriginal peoples, we look to the ways we support each other, where we purchase, where we go, and how we create enterprise. Spending money on rent is one of the ways we can work together. I contacted other major Native social organizations and asked them how much they spent on rent. It didn't take long to determine that we were paying a lot in rent without long-term return.

Our services would be improved if we were better linked. We were sending people from Mamawi [a family services organization] to other organizations for employment and training. Maybe we had an obligation to locate our services together, which would help our clientele save on bus tickets. We secured funding and hired a consultant to complete a social and situational analysis of the CP building.

The project's scale was overwhelming. It was a big building needing lots of work, but the analysis concluded the building was structurally sound and the mechanical system was old but sound. The impact analysis concluded that in terms of the community, it was important to work together in one place. Health and well-being were priorities followed by training and employment. We tried to assess whether or not to go ahead.

We hadn't done any fund-raising, and no government wanted us to do this. The provincial minister of Native Services thought it was a good idea. There was no talk, however, of support from the infrastructure program used by other cultural groups to secure community centres. We decided to go ahead and purchased the building for $1.1 million.

We went to five Aboriginal organizations and asked their boards to pass a resolution to be on the hook for $10,000 each. We made the offer to purchase with funds from those resolutions and from the city and the federal department of National Historic Sites and Monuments. We had enough to purchase the building and operate it for several months at a cost of $8,000 per month for heat and electricity."

Discussions arose in the community about the project, including the long-term viability and risk associated with investing in a large building versus directing efforts to funding other projects and programs on a smaller scale. In any event, the Aboriginal Centre of Winnipeg, Inc. (ACWI) was incorporated in 1990 as a non-profit organization, and the historic CP building was purchased in December 1992. A board of directors was elected, and restoration work was begun. ACWI members, who applied and met the criteria of being an Aboriginal organization, purchased shares and then incorporated ACWI Heritage Corp. It is a registered charity that facilitates the fund-raising activities of supporters for additional restoration and operation of a large rotunda area suitable for public events. The decision to renovate an existing building is in direct support of sustainable development initiatives that reuse and recycle available resources.

Bill stepped into his position and saw that his mandate was to accomplish three goals. He had to manage risk one step at a time. His first priority was the physical building. Hiring a building maintenance engineer set things in motion. His second priority was to develop a business plan and an architectural development plan in order to secure funding. Finally, the administration of the project was secured by setting up an office in the Aboriginal Centre. Bill's case study (1997) of the Aboriginal Centre provides more insight into the purchase and refurbishing project.

A major retro-fit of the building was required, but there were no funds to do the work. Wayne recalls their strategy to make leasing space available:

There is a little program available through Unemployment Insurance where people work, do not get paid but they maintain their benefits. The sponsor gets $100 per week to get hammers and nails. We took sixty Aboriginal men and women into this program. We got them to tear down walls and clean up. We saved over a million dollars. Then funding was secured to upgrade the building to meet fire regulations.

One of our stipulations to the contractors who were bidding was that 70 per cent of their workforce had to be Aboriginal peoples. They said that they couldn't meet that requirement. We insisted that they consider the sixty people who had demonstrated some capacity in the previous project. When this upgrading project was finished, we came in under budget and had an average of 90 per cent Aboriginal employment.

This project provided the opportunity to work together beyond government programs, which the system does not encourage. Wayne notes that they had to operate from a place of equivalency where differences didn't matter. They avoided talk of division, such as seniority issues, and instead tried to cooperate.

Wayne shares some thoughts for others trying to undertake projects involving major cooperation:

It is hard to give advice, because in many ways it is timing. The resources came together, and we didn't compromise. The cycle will come back around, and if not now, then it will be a good project later on.

The vision was for inclusivity. Stick to that, or you will start to die or at least sink. We had a funder who wanted to give funds for only one group in opposition to our philosophy. It was hard because we needed the funds but we did not compromise. We all had a vision for a good future, and that helped us to stay on track.

We considered the political ramifications of the project. We didn't ask permission of the non-Aboriginal government so we didn't ask permission of the quasi-Aboriginal government groups. We informed them. We kept them on-line. We always invited their participation. I met with the leaders who were informed but not active. We tried to focus on the business aspects too. It makes sense to pay a reasonable rent and be accessible to your clients. There is a sustaining benefit that goes to the organization that is not there if they are just paying rent. We encouraged having more responsibility and control over the property.

The support for projects can come many ways. Sometimes I would rather have somebody's commitment then somebody's money. We have shown that the fears that many bureaucrats have need not come true. I was told that one politician received advice when first approached by the group that here was another Indian group with a big idea when half of them run off with the money or half of them won't perform or they don't have the experience. We have the experience and we know better.

This lack of support persists today. I am told by some senior officials who are non-Aboriginal and who really believe that now we can do things, that people are nice to your face or they want to argue with you but they won't. I like the people who will challenge us because those are the ones who will ultimately make you stronger anyway. It's the ones who don't seem to have an opinion except in other circles such as those cocktail parties where we're kind of laughed at. We have to stay strong.

The most gratifying thing was to see the people who came with substance-abuse problems or who are working off fines under the fine option program, and they have become so committed to the project that it restores their lives. I see them doing anything they need to make it work. It is gratifying because I don't know where they would be without this project. Their lives are so much more productive.

Be persistent. Be clear in vision, simple and inclusive. Be specific about your expectations and be prepared to answer questions. There is a certain distinction where we have to do things our way and know the rules of how to play the game. Hold onto your priorities, but know how to accommodate the people you need.

The Aboriginal Centre of Winnipeg provides focus for the community, and many of the original organizers continue to provide consistent leadership, facilitating project viability and success. Many organizations that operate from locations throughout the city are integrated into the community. The centre provides an alternative that is also welcomed. The variety of services located there range from employment and training, family services, and language preservation to artists' workspace, communication services, and women's advocacy. This project meets the objective of locating key services at the convenience of clients.

The project is financially successful, although there is still controversy around the suitability of focusing so many resources on real estate rather than the major concern of programs. Dissenting voices provide the opportunity for underlying rationale to be revisited and improvements made if necessary. Loxley (2000) does have concerns about centralization of services especially since relying substantially on public moneys results in higher risk than is necessary for a project such as this. Care must be taken to further strengthen the centre's financial viability. The project's impact has been far-reaching in the Aboriginal community, Bill notes: "A significant piece of property is now owned by Aboriginal organizations. There are extensive opportunities for education and training in the Aboriginal Centre. Employment opportunities, business-support services are available, as well as government, administrative, and business services in a convenient location."

The only political group located at the centre is the Aboriginal Council of Winnipeg. This group is the subject of the next section as an organization specifically targeting urban Aboriginal residents.

POLITICAL REPRESENTATION: ABORIGINAL COUNCIL OF WINNIPEG

The Aboriginal Council of Winnipeg (ACW) was formed in 1990 by the amalgamation of two organizations that served the needs of urban-based Aboriginal peoples. One was the Urban Indian Association and the other was the Winnipeg Council of Treaty and Status Indians. The rationale was that an urban-based organization would be most effective in supporting the rights of Aboriginal peoples living in Winnipeg. Artificial legal distinctions bind the activities of many Aboriginal organizations that focus on only one group such as First Nations or Métis. ACW tries to bridge distinctions by focusing on the Aboriginal heritage of its members and not on specific group membership.

Up to that point, negotiations of any significance involved the Assembly of Manitoba Chiefs, the Manitoba Métis Federation, and the provincial or federal government. There was no mechanism for putting forward the concerns of urban Aboriginal peoples. ACW stepped in to meet this need. "We would not allow government to divide us," says Mary Richard, ACW president (personal communication, 1997). "We were Aboriginal tax-payers, and we had to be given recognition for our own. If I walked down the street, who cared if I had a number or not? I was an Indian, and we were all in the same boat. It does not take a lot of money, as we only get $44,000 per year from the province."

In the mid-1990s, self-government talks were underway, but again without any significant input from the urban population. Mary's focus shifted to making sure that urban needs were voiced in the proper forums. She met with the leadership in Aboriginal organizations and in organizations that serve an Aboriginal clientele, in order to educate them about the need to participate in the process of self-government. "I told them that the federal government had a policy on self government and that if we did not get involved, the policy would be implemented, and without any input from us," Mary recalls. "We called a meeting of all these groups and met with over one hundred people and discussed priorities for Winnipeg self-government."

At the same time, ACW was developing a network of supporters with city council and the province of Manitoba. AMC and MMF declined to be involved, since ACW did not represent every Aboriginal person in Winnipeg, although MMF did attend the prioritization session. This is an indication of the tension that exists between the organizations as AMC and MMF determine how they might best represent their urban-based members.

Mary demonstrates her leadership philosophy in facing this criticism and in the way she works to accomplish the goals of ACW: "I just don't pay attention to those kind of things. I keep going," she says. "When the people say we want to do something, then ACW does it. I don't care if there are five or ten people. If I deal with five people, then they know five more people, and the circle gets bigger and soon there are fifty people. My background is community development so we work to make people aware of the situation by planning with them. We strategize with them, provide training, and help them carry out their plans."

The goals of ACW focus on issues that affect urban-based Aboriginal peoples. ACW acts as a forum for discussion of all issues and promotes the development of new and positive directions. It is concerned with the culture, interests, lives, and identity of Winnipeg's Aboriginal peoples. Racism and prejudice are targets of education programs within the context of promoting harmonious race relations with all Winnipeggers. Many Aboriginal peoples face the same problems in the city. They have no land base, they are scattered throughout the city with some concentration in the inner city, and many of their children have little or no connection to their families' home communities.

The leadership of any organization affects the way it accomplishes its goals. ACW is no exception. Mary Richard and ACW vice-president George Munroe have philosophies that significantly influence the organization's success in meeting these goals. The board prioritizes particular projects with membership input in order to accomplish ACW's goals. These projects include a memorandum of agreement, nurturing initiatives, the Neeginan project, and support of youth.

With the poor representation of urban Aboriginal peoples that was previously mentioned, a memorandum of understanding (MOU) was a priority. "We recently signed a tripartite agreement with the federal,

provincial, and municipal governments that gives us a little more authority to be able to speak to the different levels of government,"
George states. "The agreement gives us access to the federal and provincial governments, who we did not have access to before, in a legal
sense. Before, they tolerated us, but now they have signed an MOU
agreement, so they have to deal with us. They were not willing to deal
with us up until a few months ago. It is taking to time to change."

It is a unique agreement that has the potential to give a voice to urban concerns when federal or provincial organizations and departments come together. ACW's standing is formalized, and it is hoped that
the Aboriginal peoples of Winnipeg will benefit.

In addition to the MOU, a number of projects have their genesis with
and/or support of ACW. Mary notes that the organization is not interested in controlling anyone since their job is to help people to think for
themselves. They do not take anything away from the people they
work with because it is important to have the opportunity to do things
within their own group. ACW steps out of their way so they can take
over. This is a significant philosophy for encouraging capacity building
and a sustainable approach for building a strong community.

ACW is a political organization and a special interest group. They do
not provide services to their members. Instead one strategy they follow
is that they broker their political clout to the benefit of projects that
help urban Aboriginal peoples. Playing a role akin to the United Way,
ACW encourages groups to remain autonomous while benefiting from
ACW's fund-raising expertise until self-sufficiency is achieved and
projects do not require ACW's support.

According to Mary, young people are actively involved. "We don't
allow Aboriginal Council, MMF [Manitoba Métis Federation], and AMC
[Assembly of Manitoba Chiefs] politics to get in the way of our youth.
I just step out of the way, and they can negotiate better than I can."

George identifies other successful strategies:

We have been able to talk with the three levels of government without dividing
our community or categorizing the problem into a federal or a provincial concern. We speak to the government about problems that face all Aboriginal peoples, including poor housing, unemployment, gaming, poverty, and many
others. We face them together as a community rather than get into different jurisdictional issues.

By and large, we have been successful. One of the things I like about the
council is that whether the government or anybody else approves of what we

are doing, the authority comes from our constituent members who gather together at different times of the year and tell us to go ahead. We started with
having a good relationship with the grassroots, which is the basis for everything that we have done.

It is also important to have the non-Aboriginal community working with
you and working behind you. We have been very successful in making inroads
with the Chamber of Commerce, city council, and the chief of police. We meet
with different ethnic communities in the city.

The organizational structure has nine elected members and an elder.
The president and vice-president work full time for ACW, their personal incomes augmented by consulting work, and then each member holds a
portfolio ranging from women's issues, business development, and justice
to children, employment, and the penitentiaries. Terms range from one to
three years. Community consultation is the backbone of ACW's approach.

When an issue arises, advice is sought from the community and implemented by ACW. George recounts an issue with an elder who was
abusing his authority. "He was alleged to have sexually abused some
young girls at a youth centre, and charges were laid against him. We
called a meeting with the elders and said, Look, how do we prevent
stuff like this from happening? It reflects on us as a community. So they
suggested that we set up a council of elders that will deal with any issues having to deal with elders. They will deal with their peers rather
than having outside people dealing with the issue. So we set up a council of fourteen elders from different parts of the community in Manitoba. Whenever issues come up that have to deal with tradition,
culture, or history such as abuse of power and authority of elders, then
the elders council deals with it."

Consensus-building is an important part of determining a direction
for ACW that will benefit the community. An issue is introduced at a
meeting and then members break into smaller groups to discuss it. Everyone voices an opinion, and the group opinion is identified and
shared with the gathering.

"We know it is impossible to make everyone happy," George observes
"We don't vote and try to get 51 per cent, because we are never going to get
it anyway. We take the consensus from each group, and generally there is
an agreement that this feels right for the community to be going in a particular direction. We have had tremendous success in using that approach."

The contribution of every member, especially women and youth, is
important. From board work to office administration, their work is ap-

preciated. ACW deals with issues of poverty, unemployment, and lack of training that have long dogged Aboriginal peoples, but today these problems have changed in intensity. Several decades ago, gangs were not a concern. The groundwork for these criminal activities was laid by the community's dysfunction. George says that people do not realize the kind of cross-country struggle that he and others are involved in, both in rural and urban settings. One question that has arisen is the need to focus on being more representative of the urban Aboriginal population by building a stronger member base and enhancing the organization's credibility.

According to George, it was twenty-five years ago that he and other community members recognized this dysfunction and the division in the community. In order to deal with it, the Neeginan project was conceived, but initially funding could not be found for it. ACW has picked it up so many years later to reinterpret it and make it a reality. George recalls Neeginan's original premise:

In order for us to deal effectively with all the social and economic problems facing our community, we decided that we were going to come up with more comprehensive plans. Neeginan was born. We included housing, economic development issues, social services, education, and training, and employment. We had to put it together in a way that was going to deal effectively with these problems in a major way, and that is how Neeginan developed originally. That was what we were looking at twenty-five years ago.

Today it is still involves total community development. It is housing, economic development, social services, education, and spiritual and cultural development. The anchor is the spiritual and cultural centre that we are building right on the corner of Higgins and Main Street. From there will radiate all the other developments in phases.

The ACW leadership changed in an election in 1999. For George and Mary, ACW needs to stay in touch with the community. It is important to help people get their dreams of a program or service to the community off the ground but then to step aside so they can carry on. That independence brings the greatest satisfaction. Passion for making change is important. The rate of change will continue and perhaps accelerate as it is expressed in a productive manner.

The Aboriginal community's support for ACW will have to move to financial support so that ACW's voice is strong and not compromised by reliance on outside funding. ACW must remain inclusive and minimize divisions in the community for whatever reason.

The move to new leadership after the election has not been smooth, but Sean Kocsis, the new president, wants to build on the work of previous administrations and build membership to a point that truly represents Aboriginal peoples in Winnipeg.

ACW has a proud history that its members clearly hope will continue. The nurturing of young leaders by those who have experience is important in a sustainable approach to building a strong organization and community. This is in keeping with Aboriginal tradition and ensures strong leadership through new ideas and training while holding onto significant history.

Besides the issue of leadership transition, issues have arisen around the roles that AMC, MMF, and ACW will play in the lives of urban-based Aboriginal peoples. Those roles continue to evolve, based on membership for AMC and MMF, and location for ACW. ACW meets the needs of all urban-based Aboriginal peoples regardless of where they come from.

Another part of the dream of a hub of Aboriginal activity in the north end has been the development of a business centre. The Aboriginal Business Development Centre is reviewed in the next section.

BUILDING CAPACITY:
ABORIGINAL BUSINESS DEVELOPMENT CENTRE

Starting Point

The Aboriginal Business Development Centre (ABDC) is located in the Aboriginal Centre. Its board of directors includes Sean Kocsis, a lawyer and business consultant, and Len Flett, vice-president for The North West Company. Len brings significant retail experience in the North, and Sean has worked with many Aboriginal communities in Manitoba. Both bring to the ABDC knowledge and sensitivity to the needs of their own people.

Len (personal conversation, 1998) recalls the early dreams regarding a business development centre:

Our vision was to clean up the image of that particular area, mainly because our own people were involved in it, and the image of Winnipeg was the image of you and me. We figured that when we put all of the organizations into one location, the economic impact would start to radiate from that particular centre, and a lot of other businesses would be attracted there. A hotel and restaurants would want to take advantage of the new economy that was developing there. A ripple was what we were looking for, and it is starting to happen. The Aboriginal Centre and the proposed Neeginan development project including the roundhouse and other business projects make it very timely to have an Aboriginal business centre.

The target for the business centre is new entrepreneurs with the business centre itself coordinating and providing information. The ABDC will be a place where business people can go and get information and assistance with business plans and advice for business loans and so on. We are looking at an incubator system so new businesses can locate right in the office. The biggest issue will likely be breaking into mainstream markets so opportunities for Aboriginal peoples are maximized.

The ABDC is a program of the Aboriginal Council of Winnipeg. We do not have the support of any other Aboriginal political organization since they have different mandates and different constituencies. That has never been a problem, because overall we do have public support. The migration of people from the northern reserves is not going to stop. The reserves can't support the growing population. People are going to migrate from the reserve to the city and back to the reserve again because Winnipeg cannot provide all the jobs and training they are looking for.

The main problem right now is that people are migrating from the reserves with absolutely no preparation for securing jobs or entering into the job market. While people do the best they can with what they have, the ABDC may be able to help young people especially, until these same services are established in the communities.

When the need for someone to head ABDC was not easily met, Sean was invited by the rest of the board to step in and make sure the project was on its feet and running in the black. He agreed to look after the organization in early 1999. A proposal had been accepted by the Western Diversification Fund, which provides the majority of their operating funds.

In reflecting on his experiences with First Nations communities, Sean (personal communication, 1999) sees a number of challenges that must be overcome:

We're handicapped to a large extent because we lack capacity – the skill base. We use a model that is foreign to us – it is like putting a round peg into square hole. The result is that government is not as efficient or as effective as it could be, had we had our own models to begin with. We have few role models who are successful.

I worked for an individual who is a successful self-made millionaire. You would probably see very little difference if you compared him to a self-made millionaire in mainstream. The bottom line is very important, the work ethic is essential, and the results are almost all that matters.

Bottom-line driven is fine, but there is a downside, because there is abrasive and aggressive behaviour that sometimes comes with it which doesn't fit well in small communities with high unemployment. I think he has paid a high price personally because his style doesn't fit. He is a generous man so I think that he has given a lot to the community, but it is more than he has gotten back.

Sean's approach is to make his own organization run as efficiently and effectively as possible. The mixing of social and business objectives does not work at ABDC nor at another organization where he is president of the board of directors. The Andrews Street Family Centre's social objectives are partially funded by its successful catering business; it abides by proper business procedures and maintains the social/business split. Sean's experience with this organization has been very rewarding:

I am most proud of the Andrews Street Family Centre [ASFC]. It is a tight, efficiently run organization that produces measurable results where the community is happy and the funders are ecstatic. We are under review twenty-four hours a day. We never block or obscure that viewing, so the funders can come in and see the books at any time. We go through operational and management audits on a regular basis, and the ASFC passes with flying colours time after time.

The ASFC board wanted a president who had business experience, and board members with specific expertise. It is a very social-service oriented organization for the mostly Aboriginal families in the area, but they do have to generate income. They had a catering company that is now back on track. It operates efficiently following business guidelines.

The board and I allowed an environment to develop where positive things could move forward. No dishonesty, only integrity and the truth among the board and between staff which is key. We encourage risk-taking, without penalty. Positive-reinforcement recognition systems have been put in place: personal evaluation reporting systems, a picture board for public acknowledgment of hard-working staff, and staff retreats tied to performance. The number of incidents that warrant reward is increasing.

When wastage was a problem, no one had any reason to point it out. The common attitude was that people are trying their best and that is good enough. But when you are in a business, then it is not good. Errors have to be pointed out, and eventually tolerance for errors has to decrease. That has happened. Wastage has dropped considerably.

Service Delivery

As with any organization reliant on external funding, ABDC looks to meeting the terms of its funding agreement without forgetting its purpose: to facilitate and promote the development of Aboriginal business. To that end, the business centre does not want to reflect a bureaucratic atmosphere for clients who come in for assistance. Instead, it is as user-friendly as possible. Aboriginal clients meet with Aboriginal staff. They may consult for as long as it takes, including after hours, and if weekends are more convenient, then accommodating appointments are made. Clients may live in the city or they may be on reserve and looking for the type of information available from ABDC. The centre is also becoming an information source for community events.

The staff of four and between ten and thirteen volunteers meet high standards in their quality of work and their work ethic. Sean notes that the community volunteers have been invaluable: "Without the volunteers, this organization would not exist, literally. It's the volunteers who made this place survive when there was no funding. Volunteers meet our new clients and give them a tour and an introduction to the centre. They also answer phones, do typing, review proposals, and advocate on our behalf." Sean dedicates seven days a week to the centre and so is readily available for clients seeking his level of expertise on their first visit. He must demonstrate to his funders the demand for ABDC's services and, more importantly, inspire confidence in the community.

Start-up occurred in early 1999. By April, ABDC had served eight clients. In November alone, staff and volunteers saw 109 clients. They have experienced steady growth without an advertising budget, relying on word of mouth and poster displays in common areas. Their current rate of business has stretched the capacity of their human resources almost to the limit. A recent staff addition has helped to ease the load.

Most mainstream service providers deal with clients who have at least their high-school diploma, some idea of business, and a good idea of what they want to do in a business. ABDC's clients are in the pre-business phase and are building capacity through the centre's personal assistance. Sean explains:

Our client tends to have little or no high school, with three or four clients who are totally illiterate. We're starting from behind. If you have a good idea but you don't have the wherewithal to read or write, then it is very difficult. There are exceptions. One lady who is illiterate started a janitorial service for cleaning homes and offices. Generally, our client has less education and no knowledge whatsoever of business and tends to come from a background where business role models were missing.

If you are unaccustomed to working fourteen or fifteen hour days without pay, seven days a week, the culture shock is often enough to cause the idea to fail. We hand hold, counsel, and provide a range of services that cannot be found at any other service provider. It is the pre-business service that you don't find anywhere else. We have to [provide it] because our clients' ideas would fail.

Sean explains his perception of "success":

The government funder's definition of success is numerical: How many numbers of people do we serve? How many businesses were created, and how many employees were hired? The trouble with that approach is that they don't look at it in a time frame.

Another question might be: Are those people we served a year ago still employed? Otherwise it becomes a numbers race with other service providers as opposed to a race for a better-quality approach.

Since we are doing well, we have flexibility to create a new measurement. We broaden the definition of success because we also ask: How much time do we actually spend with a person? We could just spend ten minutes, but that won't meet the needs of our clients. We have people who are totally illiterate with no sense of the uphill battle they face. After a lengthy discussion they begin to realize that. Three clients have acknowledged their weaknesses and gone back to school. In many respects, this is a total success, because it is capacity building.

Finally, another way to measure success is to track jobs and businesses for one year and see if they are still in business. This tracking system needs staff, so we can't use it. It would, however, add another dimension to measuring success.

We track the numbers of clients served, businesses started, and jobs created, and we note the amount of time we spend with a client.

ABDC's success stories include business owners who have expanded their businesses. Others have started businesses that failed, but a number of them will start other ventures because of the learning experience. Many learn lessons on the job. Women and youth are comfortable using the centre's resources. For those wanting direction, they can scrutinize a list of successful and affordable business ideas that cost $500 or less to start.

Community Interest

At this point in ABDC's development, board membership was being revisited. From Sean's perspective, strong business acumen would make the difference for ABDC's success. It must be driven by its mandate and be held accountable to its members. A strategic planning session was planned to help focus activities. The annual general meeting was to be opened to any Aboriginal person to maintain a strong grassroots orientation.

The federal government has been supportive of the centre, and a strong case has been made for continued funding. However, Sean comments on the impact of the environment at the Aboriginal Centre where ABDC is located: "Numbers are fine and funders have been very happy, but they don't like the politics. We are in an environment, particularly in this building, that is very politics-rich. Any program that does well is seen enviously. We are not rich, but we work hard to make our area presentable. We set very high standards. Politics has entered into this arena, and our funders have heard that, and they are concerned. They wonder whether this program will be able to demonstrate its past record in a politically rich environment."

This kind of tension is not uncommon between programs, individuals, and families in Aboriginal communities. It is often a key factor that subverts effective capacity-building (people leave) and consistency in leadership (people leave). Community cohesiveness is affected. How can dissent be handled so that relationships survive the inevitable disagreements? It is challenging, but maintaining open lines of communication is critial.

Future

The original funding agreement asked that ABDC be self-sufficient in three years. This was unrealistic; similar service-providers in the mainstream do not face a similar constraint. If anything, ABDC has a strong position that their clientele deserve a big helping hand and a secure future. Sean predicts steady growth for the centre. He states:

There needs to be an increase in the number of Aboriginal businesses for true economic growth for Aboriginal peoples. ABDC is a necessary service providing education, training, and business advice. Where should we focus? Many people that are coming here are in pre-business. Should we focus on them, or should we focus on two or three of the real winners and make sure that they win and they win big? Our resources are stretched, and if we try to provide everything to everybody, we will fail.

If we do focus, then we cut out a whole section of people who need us. Right now we can serve anyone who comes in the door. These questions will be determined by the board in a strategic planning session. Networking with other organizations is going to be critical. For example, if the Canadian Council for Aboriginal Business invites their members to mentor our clients, then we will facilitate it. The future need is strong for ABDC. People are excited.

Len Flett agrees that the Business Centre needs to grow. His vision for ABDC sees expansion into financial services. "The whole project will also take root in its community. You are going to see a vibrant Aboriginal business community in that particular part of the city that will be a showcase for the city as a whole." ABDC has set the stage for a viable, effective vehicle for building capacity, new businesses, and employment and increasing the flow of capital through the Aboriginal community.

It is important to note these expectations. However, other factors including politics, timing of challenges, and changing leadership resulted in the ABDC closing a year later. The need for such support still continues.

The last group that will be explored is the contribution by youth to making a strong community.

BUILDING FOR THE FUTURE: ABORIGINAL YOUTH WITH INITIATIVE, INC. (AYWI)

Concern over crimes related to gangs of young people was on the rise in 1996. A call for action brought responses from many sectors, including the community's young people. A series of forums drew on young people's opinions, resulting in a better understanding of their vision for a more productive future.

A youth council was one strategy in which young people could be involved. AYWI evolved from that year of effort to provide other organizations with the youth perspective as well as to develop programs to help youth surmount the obstacles they face, through educating on process, developing capacity and commitment, and bringing a fresh energy and perspective to helping youth.

AYWI's mandate is to network and build strength with the organizations that have an impact on Aboriginal peoples in the areas of justice, education, policy, and economics. In late 1997 a group of young people were trying to make a difference. Lawrence Angeconeb, the coordinator, was then twenty-one years old. He had taken part in several local and national youth groups and had skills in Aboriginal community development. Heather Milton was the assistant coordinator. She had done community work for about three years in Winnipeg and in B.C. Clayton Thomas Müeller, twenty years old, handled communications and networking in the community. AYWI then shared office space with the Aboriginal Council of Winnipeg, and received support and advice from ACW.

AYWI participate when a youth perspective is required. They give input on youth matters to the Assembly of Manitoba Chiefs and the Manitoba Métis Federation. In Lawrence's opinion, it would have become more frustrating and discouraging to complete tasks for the young people functioning within AYWI without ACW's support.

Lawrence has been involved with groups where the timing was not right because of external crises (Oka in 1990) or lack of funding. Now funding is available because of the attention and priority given to youth issues. AYWI's initial budget was $90,000, with three staff and five volunteers. The start-up year was expensive, with office computer and supplies eating a large portion of the budget.

Initial priorities have been to contact organizations in the areas of policy, justice, economy, and education and to establish linkages. If young people have to go to one of these organizations, AYWI wants to assist them in getting the help they need and to share resources with the organizations. Heather (personal communication, 1997) describes the positive reception to AYWI: "It has been a really good response. Every organization we have talked to is amazed by our youth and what we are doing. Like, it's gone over really well. Like, it will totally fly."

Effectiveness

Identifying the ways that AYWI is productive is important for those who want to build on AYWI's compelling experience.

Involving young people   It is a challenge to meet young people and engage them. Clayton knows that he has to break through a common barrier in which young people listen to what everyone else is saying and do not contribute. This means educating them on the opportunities they have and giving them options to help them get out of a rut.

He also faces the obstacle of convincing people that young people have a part to play. This is a partnership that must be sold to different generations, both in organizations and in families. Parents must sign membership forms for children under sixteen. This gets them involved by introducing them to AYWI.

Building on information   AYWI chose to build on the information collected from the youth in their community. They did not want merely to create another study on young people.

Empowering young women   A traditional balance of strength existed in Aboriginal society between men and women. Heather recognizes that much of the work empowering young women has to be done through other young women who understand their roles in the community. These roles are not often taught in the family home, thus making them difficult to identify. Youth working together can educate and empower each other.

Lawrence and Clayton recognize the power of this process. AYWI benefits when women are in leadership positions. Young women seeing strong role models are attracted to their organization.

Tradition   The clan structure provides the basis for the board of directors, which currently has seven members. Each issue that comes before the board is looked at holistically. Board members each brings the gift of their clan or their particular expertise to the discussion. In that way, the best decision is arrived at for AYWI.

The message to youth   AYWI's message is: Get involved and make a difference. Clayton feels that trying to educate young people on how to become involved in determining their futures is critical. "I would be very choked if I could have played a part in determining my future but didn't" (personal communication, 1997).

Formal education and practical experience is the best blend, each element contributing to a young person's future success.

Messages to Other Youth Groups

AYWI gives staff the opportunity to meet and work with people in various organizations throughout the community. Many messages go out to young people thinking of starting similar community groups. The following thoughts fall out of AYWI's experience:

• Commit your plans to paper, but, as Clayton suggests, "Don't limit yourself to what is written on paper and what one person thinks you know." Build networks of people who support your work. As you get everyone's opinion and build consensus, work at seeing how it fits together.
• Celebrate the gifts of each person who has a part in the organization. Diversity has to be celebrated. Many forces will try to divert you from your goals, but the secret is to get back on your path and minimize the diversions. Lawrence says you can't take anyone or anything for granted, because if you do, it may be one of the greatest opportunities you have missed.
• Become resilient in your work. Discouragement is always there in anything that you do. Understand it as a process of learning from each mistake.
• Don't duplicate services, projects, or efforts if possible. Instead, get involved in any workshop, process, or project that supports your objectives and share resources, encouraging a sustainable approach to making a difference in the community.
• Encourage your staff and volunteers in ways that let them know their contributions are appreciated and take care that communication is open and frequent. Reaching young people requires a thoughtful style, given that it is young people talking to young people. Focus on the common ground and not diverse opinions. You can build something useful on the common ground.

No one will hand you things on a silver platter. "You have to go out and grab it, drag it, and pull it towards you," Clayton emphasizes. "Work hard for it. Nothing comes easy in life. You can't sit around all day waiting for opportunities to happen – you've got to go out and create those opportunities. Good things will happen when you work hard." Don't give up.

Future Plans

Lawrence and Heather identify youth employment issues as AYWI's future focus. Lawrence hopes that AYWI will offer employment opportunities. Heather notes that dealing with employment issues will address economic issues that are at the heart of many problems for today's young people:

The economy is the base for all communities and where our communities historically fall apart. We were all colonized, and they took away our system of trading, which was our economy.

I look at all of these young people who have all of these brilliant ideas but are not high-school educated. I think that it is very important to utilize them, because they are so brilliant and they think so broadly and moderately compared to the generation before. I want to hire all of these people and have them do something that makes them feel good about themselves.

My own personal goal is to look after my family. It is my responsibility to look after my family before I look after the community. I understand that I look after my personal life, then my family, my community, and then my nation.

Clayton's focus is on developing a network of youth across the country: take AYWI's structure and then encourage youth to use it as a model so more people get involved.

AYWI is striving for financial self-reliance, as part of their self-sustaining goal. It was their dream to generate enough revenues to support their programs shortly after the first year. This might be through consultative fees with business and non-profit sectors or through nominal membership fees. Building an organization that becomes self-sustaining takes time and commitment. Youthful enthusiasm is critical, but limited resources may be difficult to access, so the question arises how successful AYWI will be in facing these challenges over the long term.

AYWI is supported by young people who are dedicated to making a difference for their peers. They have the advantage of their youth, persistence, and membership in the community they are trying to serve. They face the struggle of motivating their volunteers for a sustained period of time and securing financial support. Their network of supporters will be a great asset in those periods when progress seems minimal or even "two giant steps back." Their advice for other youth groups is based on their experience and freely given to the community. AWYI seems to have everything they need to make a difference. Their parting words are, "We will succeed."

SUMMARY

Nurturing cohesive, supportive community in an urban setting is a tough proposition. Winnipeg's Aboriginal community is visionary and tenacious. The provincial government has been supportive in securing an urban Aboriginal strategy based on extensive public consultation. Both federal and provincial governments were involved in funding the

Aboriginal Centre, the Aboriginal Council of Winnipeg, the Aboriginal Business Development Centre, and the Aboriginal Youth With Initiative. These dollars help to take dreams down the path to reality.

The past five years has seen many, many changes to this portrait of Winnipeg's dynamic Aboriginal community. Each of the projects and organizations has met community needs in ways that reflect the experience of the leadership and targeted membership. Community members in all walks of life have continued to support one or more of these groups. Many of the public meetings that might be called in the course of a year are well-attended or even overflowing with interested participants, evidence of building strong organizations and community. However, the drive to build a core of activity to spark the community has had mixed results.

The Aboriginal Centre houses many organizations, but many others do not operate from that base. This mirrors the reality of living in an urban centre where the Aboriginal community is spread out. Development builds on previous experience. It is very difficult to meet everyone's needs using a centralized approach when a decentralized approach may be more effective. The Aboriginal Centre will continue to be part of the hub of community activity, given its central role in the Neeginan project. The centre has some controversy associated with it and the high risk it represents, but it is proving its viability each year that it remains in operation. Its boards and executive are filled with individuals with years of experience and years of education. Some are newer to the Winnipeg scene than others. Their effectiveness depends to some extent on how political motivations colour their activities. For those able to bridge varying backgrounds and differences of opinion, leadership has a positive relationship with successful development decisions.

ACW has a solid record of working with the urban community. That community will decide who best represents them, given the competition between AMC (Manitoba Métis Federation), MMF (the Assembly of Manitoba Chiefs), and ACW. ACW leadership was in transition, but it had experience in the previous leadership to draw on to take advantage of all its assets and new leadership with a vision to support. ABDC was building on a strong foundation of service and support of potential entrepreneurs and business owners, both on and off reserve. It tried to meet a need that is unique to the Aboriginal community for insightful support to particular needs of new entrepreneurs with less education and previous training, in an effort at capacity building. The wheels were in motion for a successful organization that in the end didn't continue; but much can still be learned.

AYWI proved an excellent training ground for young people to further their education and take up other opportunities with organizations making a difference to society. Its efforts supported a strong community that was sustainably developing its talent, and it operated successfully for several years, when it became part of the AMC's youth department. The staff wanted it to work and were committed to making it happen. Their voices will continue to be heard.

SEEKING BALANCE
AND PROSPERITY

4

Toquaht First Nation, British Columbia

TOQUAHT FIRST NATION is a tiny community with fish and forest resources. It has a strong traditional background, with hereditary chief Burt Mack holding a lifetime position. Chief Mack has demonstrated entrepreneurial strengths in running band-owned businesses including a sawmill, lumber operation, clam farm, and other seafood harvesting enterprises and in supporting local small-business people. Chief Mack's family owns a bookstore and art gallery. The West Coast approach to tradition is very evident in this community.

TRADITION, COMMUNITY, AND FAMILY

Toquaht First Nation is located near Ucluelet in British Columbia. It is one Nuu-chah-nulth (formerly Nootka) community that has maintained its governing system of hereditary chiefs. According to Neel (1992), the tribes on the West Coast traditionally had a head chief, or *ha'wiih*, and a number of sub-chiefs. While the Toquaht nation refers to them as heads of families and not sub-chiefs, these chiefs held "seats" that carried "names" and had specific responsibilities for such things as territories, rivers, and potlatching (p 21).

Judith Sayers, chief of Hupaᴄasath First Nation, a Nuu-chah-nulth community, notes that the system followed a paternal line from father to son. The *haw'iih* made decisions in consultation with his advisors and the other chiefs. The *haw'iih* had very important responsibilities, or *ha-houlthee,* for the whole territory. *Ha-houlthee* meant the *haw'iih* had responsibilities to use the land and its resources so that every person in the community was taken care of. "It was a whole system of government where people had responsibilities," Sayers explains.

"Some were beach keepers and would take care of everything along the beachfront, while some people were in charge of the rivers and would look after the streams and the fish. Forest keepers would look after the medicines, the forest plants, and clean up fallen trees. Everybody had important roles and responsibilities in our society."

Chief Bert Mack is the *haw'iih* for the Toquaht First Nation. He heads the thunderbird clan. He has a speaker, the person with the responsibility to speak for the chief. Toquaht is also one of the few Nuu-chah-nulth nations with a head of the wolf clan in the community. Chief Mack appointed this person to this powerful position based on many things including family background.

"We believe that the other society [Europeans] follow the family tree. We follow the roots," Chief Mack explains. "That is where it all comes from. My mother was the community historian, as were a few women before her. She kept all the family histories and was able to answer any crisis that might occur around our history. When you trace relationships based on generations, it does not explain who or why. The roots explain your position and who is next in line. They explain your responsibilities. That is how communities are held together."

Preparing to take up the responsibilities of the *haw'iih* began in childhood. Leaders were schooled and tutored for the time they would succeed their fathers or elders. The community is small today. Three families, Mack, Thompson, and Mackay, make up one-third of their membership of 112 people. The rest live outside the community. Chief Mack has his language and follows his culture. But besides that culture, he says, "we need to understand the other society also, because of the changing of each era ... This is what my father was always saying, 'You got to get to know both ways to get along and to understand people.' I don't know how many of the chiefs have got that idea, to try and understand both worlds" (Neel, 1992:74).

Community traditions are not secret, but there are special times when they are talked about and shared and not talked about otherwise. Chief Mack says that the wolf is a most significant animal because it lives in strong communities where members look after each other. Chief Mack's community emulates this approach. The thunderbird is a mythical bird that is also meaningful to teachings on community morality. It is of special significance to the *haw'iih*.

The Northwest coast community ceremony that Europeans labelled a "potlatch" the community knows as *klu-kwana*. Chief Mack notes that few communities follow the rules and regulations of the *klu-*

kwana any longer Prior to contact, *klu-kwana* was the constitution and influenced lifestyles. It was where the role of each person was determined: "Archie Thompson, an elder, is the designated speaker for the chief, and his family has always been by my side. The head of the wolf clan is the younger brother in the Mackay family. His older brother is the keeper of the beaches. If another tribe visits, then he directs them to the chief's private beach. The visitors come and share their mission or ask for a young lady's hand" (personal communication, 1996).

According to Neel, "The *klu-kwana* is where all these different responsibilities come from and are given as a real honour. The *klu-kwana* is the way of life, the law, the power of life – all the way from the law to the dancing culture, a lot to do with handling medicines, a lot to do with fishing, which we lived on. The whale hunters used to use it a lot in their ceremonies before they went out ... social, political, everything. It was so strong the head of the wolf clan had the power to put people to death ... That's why I term it as the constitution, because everything hinged on that – that's where everything came from" (Neel, 1992:74).

Women have important roles. Chief Mack mentioned their roles as historians, while Archie Thompson, elder and speaker, notes that women are recognized as life givers. "They look after children, and offer them unconditional love, and speak to them from the heart," he says. "I have seen when you are thinking about how much you love a child, and they turn around and give you a hug without you saying a word. That is unconditional love. We all need it, and it is very important for the young people of today." The women elders of the community make important decisions around roles and responsibilities of community members.

While wanting to understand the "new people" (Europeans), Chief Mack notes that his great-grandfather warned his son to avoid following the Indian Act. Tribal custom has been followed since then, so there are no elections.

Under the Indian Act, a chief councillor is elected every two years. In communities where there are also hereditary chiefs, the responsibilities are divided, according to Judith Sayers. Some communities acknowledge the hereditary chiefs' authority over the land, while the chief councillor handles the administrative duties and the funding from Department of Indian Affairs.

Having a chief councillor makes achieving long-term plans difficult where two years is too short a time to make a significant difference.

Chief Mack says, "I have seen where one guy has foresight about what might be done in tourism, but he was voted out. The project could have carried on, even though he was voted out, by putting him in the position of manager. The community did not do that, and the opportunity still remains for someone to start up again. They voted him back in four years later, and he still talks about the project. He won't start it himself because of the community reaction the last time."

Chief Mack sees other problems arising from the Indian Act system of leadership: "While we are very socially conscious and recognize everyone in the community, there are people who always want to get close to the chief, which creates friction. My great-grandfather anticipated that the Indian Act would demoralize all Indian nations and create a system that would give these people a chance to push the true leaders unfairly. He also thought that it would create dependence. My father refused to listen to the government people too. If there was a need for a loaf of bread, then we worked for it instead of asking for it."

This philosophy of independence encouraged a strong work ethic. Chief Mack started a company when he was eighteen. He, his brothers, and his father operated fishing boats while avoiding debt, unlike most other fishers who owed the company who bought their catch. By working hard, he and his family managed to be successful. When the fishing industry started to decline, Chief Mack moved to MacMillan Bloedel (M&B), a logging company, where he worked for thirty-two years. His father had told him that timbering was an area to investigate for a business.

By observing every move that M&B made, Chief Mack learned how to operate a timber business. "When my tribe was awarded a forestry licence, I was able to rely on my M&B experience," he says. "We are able to operate so that there is no danger of overcutting. We look after the streams, so we minimize damage to fish stocks. There was some opposition to the forestry licence in the community. I have the right, however, to make my own decisions, which I do quite often. I believe in Theodore Roosevelt's advice to walk softly and carry a big stick."

TOQUAHT NATION TODAY

Toquaht Nation is a small community with a timber licence and fishing rights. Six reserves consisting of 194.7 hectares of land comprise its land holdings. The current land question is seeking title to additional lands along with control over natural resources. With land questions secured, Chief Mack predicts, community people will feel tied to the land and will not leave where they and their forefathers were born.

Chief Mack relies on his advisors. Archie Thompson emphasizes the importance of elders in bringing balance to the decision-making process. His balance is achieved through many things, including daily prayer. Archie also acknowledges the importance of loving children unconditionally. That is a parent's responsibility, he says. "It is in the gathering together and working together that people feel strength in the community and that they are not alone."

Archie's role in the negotiations over the land question is broader than acting as speaker for Chief Mack. As an elder, his message to the rest of the Nuu-chah-nulth communities is to work together, showing respect for each other and for the house of their hosts by not displaying anger.

The Toquaht Nation has few social problems, according to Chief Mack. Education is seen as a good way to improve the standard of living. The chief's granddaughter is completing training in landscaping, and his grandson wants to go to college or university. This grandson, David Johnson, is the next link in the line of *haw'iih*. While he does not speak the language, David has indicated interest in returning to the community if they want him. He admits, however that he does not understand all the responsibilities that this position holds.

Relations with the townspeople and the "new people" are good. Chief Mack's philosophy is that it is best for the community to all work together. Gale Johnson, one of his daughters, has joined the Chamber of Commerce and notes that for the most part people there are interested in supporting each other. However, she says that some business owners incorrectly thought that native people with a business idea could go to the band office and get all the money they might need, giving them an advantage over non-Aboriginal business people.

PUSH FOR ECONOMIC DEVELOPMENT

Toquaht First Nation has tribal-owned businesses as well. Chief Mack carries on the entrepreneurial spirit. His father believed in businesses being run by community members who know that type of business best. In addition to the timber business, there is a small sawmill, a clam farm, and other seafood harvesting. Gary Johnson, Chief Mack's son-in-law, manages the timber and sawmill enterprises. A young man whose family has extensive clam-farming experience in the community has full responsibility for the clam farm.

Chief Mack and his family have owned and operated an art gallery for more than twenty years, as well as a heavy-equipment construction company for road building and a building contract company. Chief Mack's attitude has been to avoid government funding. For instance, he secured a contract and entered a lease-to-own agreement on three expensive pieces of equipment. By the end of the contract, he owned the equipment and other pieces of machinery too.

Gary Johnson has twenty-two years of experience with M&B as a development engineer. The main purpose of the forest licence is to provide a source of fibre for the sawmill, which provides employment for some Toquaht members. "The sawmill is low tech to keep costs down and to enable us to bring in unskilled people for training," he says. "The plan is to train young people and eventually bring in high-tech industries where they will be able to train on the job. We have nine employees, and five are community members. We hope to access a B.C. Forestry training program to train additional people and add a night shift to the operation. A concern for us are the threats to our supply by other companies that encroach on Toquaht traditional land. We can have a cut level up to 25,000 per year, which would last forever without these incursions."

Other business opportunities exist in the area of tourism. The forest service has asked that the community assume responsibility for operating a campground in the area, Chief Mack says. He sees in that proposal a possible opportunity for several positions in a business with healthy revenue. "In addition to the campground, there is a trailer-park with a compound for fishing boat lock-up. Responsibility for that would rest with the campground operators. The trailer-park people might want to lease boats and go fishing rather than bringing their boats. The campground is in the middle of a five-mile stretch of property that might be developed as a subdivision."

Chief Mack provides guidance and assistance to other community members interested in starting businesses. For example, two brothers started a company to build log homes. They are no longer in business, as their supply of quality logs dried up and they were not aggressive in seeking out raw material in direct competition with other companies. However new opportunities may arise for them. Chief Mack recalls, "I helped pull it together by getting markets lined up, searching out sources for logs and experts to help finish the house the way that the owner wants. I urged them to consider selling the log cabin shell. We got into some trouble because they began depending on me too much. Anyway, they can go and work for themselves or for others. They have the necessary skills."

Gale Johnson manages the art gallery and picture-framing business with her mother, who is less active in the store. They employ one person and part-time summer help. The gallery provides a showcase for local artists, which makes it attractive to tourists. Gale plans eventually to expand to include buildings where artists will work and tourists can walk through and watch. She sees this as a great opportunity to correct misinformation and share her community's stories.

FUTURE PLANS

The major problems regarding expansion or new ventures, according to Gary Johnson, are cash flow and staffing. A worker's self-worth has to be protected, and this is undermined by make-work projects. Any project must be cost-efficient and competitive. The idea is to build on the current skills and encourage those wanting to start their own businesses to do so. The focus is on providing for the community's youth and on continuing efforts to be sustainable. Further to these goals is the understanding that projects have to meet the needs of the community. For example, there are plans for a retirement project at Macoah, Toquaht's original reserve. However, an open-pit mine in a burial ground would not be supported by the elders or the community, so they would not even consider such a project.

Gale's vision is to see an opportunity to socialize with the rest of their community and to reconnect with them. She hopes that all are able to meet their personal goals for independence and to do what they want to do. With the settlement of the land question will come the opportunity for the community to identify the rules governing tribe membership. It is possible that Gale's children may not qualify for tribe membership, however, since their father is not a band member. This could have repercussions for the hereditary chieftainship.

In summary, this small community has strong traditions, of hereditary leadership and independence. Chief Mack is well aware of his responsibilities to his community within a contemporary context and blends tradition with experience. He believes in preserving community independence from the federal government and the Indian Act. He relies on his advisors in making key decisions as they pertain to the land and his community, but he will make other decisions based on his business experience and expertise. Cautious in financing new initiatives, he protects community independence by minimizing government sources of funds.

Chief Mack exercises his entrepreneurial talent and supports community members in their efforts, and he builds on the strength of local expertise in a number of tribal businesses. His family works with him in some of the family businesses. They have skills that they have brought back to the community and intend on using to build a positive future for their children. Family and community are important and meant to be nurtured and protected.

5

Tla-o-qui-aht First Nation, British Columbia

TLA-O-QUI-AHT FIRST NATION joins Toquaht First Nation and the other Nuu-chah-nulth communities involved in the long negotiations for a land claims agreement. Tla-o-qui-aht has an elected chief councillor who relies on the hereditary chiefs for guidance in this process and in other community decisions. The community is consulted thoroughly on the decisions that are being taken. Many may recall the demonstrations around logging of Clayoquot Sound. Part of this community lives on Meares Island. Their major investment is an ocean-front resort that provides employment. There are supports for business people, and several are interviewed here about their experiences.

On Vancouver Island's west coast lie the traditional lands of the Tla-o-qui-aht First Nation. This community is a member of the Nuu-chah-nulth Tribal Council (NTC) and the Central Region Board and has ten reserves located on lands around the village of Tofino and the surrounding area, a short distance from Toquaht First Nations and the village of Ucluelet. Three hundred members live primarily on two reserves, and more than 450 members live outside of their territory. It is a vital nation with a reputation based on a long history of great strength and courage. Their leaders are looked to for guidance at a time when many of the Nuu-chah-nulth community seek a joint lands claims settlement.

The primary objective of the NTC gives insight into the philosophy of governance that affects Tla-o-qui-aht. The council focuses on economic, social, physical, and cultural development for its membership and takes full responsibility for their destinies, survival, and well-being. This responsibility is claimed in the same way that they claim the stature their communities once enjoyed in controlling their affairs on a local and regional basis. They seek meaningful coexistence and cooperation with their neighbours which will be achieved when their values and existence are respected by those neighbours (Nuu-chah-nulth Tribal Council, 1998).

Part of the process for reclaiming control of territories involves an extensive land-claims process. Thirteen Nuu-chah-nulth communities have joined in this process, which generated an Interim Measures Agreement in 1994 and a Nuu-chah-nulth Framework Agreement in 1996. In 1997, in the fourth stage of a six-stage negotiation process, the focus was on the Agreement-in-Principle. It was not an easy process, with the pressure to hurry competing with the desire to fully discuss and gain meaningful input from community members. The full implications were difficult to predict and were not helped by the legal language employed by the government.

Leaders, elders, and community members regularly convened to plan their strategy prior to negotiations with the government. Massive time commitments were required to ensure the process was successful for their communities and for future generations. This left little time to handle their other responsibilities as the hereditary and elected leaders of their communities. Human resources were stretched thinly across many areas of concern, requiring sacrifice and personal strength. Tradition was a great source of comfort and a grounding in this time of turbulence and pressure.

A project completed in March 1995 by the Clayoquot Sound Scientific Panel combined the knowledge of local elders and the scientific community relating to forest practices. It identified several critical principles affecting Nuu-chah-nulth approaches to resource management. Respect for all living things as sacred gifts, encapsulated in the phrase *hishuk ish ts´awalk* (everything is one), is explained by Roy Haiyupus:

Nothing is isolated from other aspects of life surrounding it and within it. This concept is the basis for the respect for nature that our people live with, and also contributed to the value system that promoted the need to be thrifty, not to be wasteful, and to be totally conscious of our actual needs in the search for foods. The idea and practices of over-exploitation are deplorable to our people. The practice is outside our realm of values ... Respect for nature requires a healthy state of stewardship with a healthy attitude ... respect the spiritual ... respect and conserve are key values. (Scientific Panel for Sustainable Forest Practices in Clayoquot Sound, 1995:6)

Other related principles celebrate the interconnectedness of life and a long-term commitment to sustainability integral to long-term harmony. Finally, cultural, spiritual, social, and economic well-being is essential to that harmony (6).

Regaining comprehensive harmony is tied to NTC's objective of regaining the status that was once held by the community. Prior to the arrival of the Europeans, the Nuu-chah-nulth exercised absolute authority. The hereditary chiefs, or *haw'iih*, made decisions in consultation with their advisors and other chiefs. The *haw'iih* had very important responsibilities (*ha-houlthee*) for the whole territory. *Ha-houlthee* meant that the *haw'iih* had responsibilities to use the land and its resources so that every person in the community was taken care of: "Within Ha-houlthee lies the key to the social and cultural practices, tribal membership and property ownership, economic, environmental and resource controls to promote effective enhancement levels to sustain life for the tribe today and for generations to come" (9). This traditional way of life continues to serve as a source of inspiration and guidance throughout the land claims process.

UNDERSTANDING THE COMMUNITY

Chief Francis Frank, a social worker by training, has been the elected chief councillor for five consecutive terms. He is involved in the claims process with his hereditary chiefs, advisors, and councillors. While Tla-o-qui-aht elects councillors every two years, this has not displaced the hereditary chiefs. The elected councillors handle the administration of the community but look to the community for guidance and consensus on the direction for their community.

"We carried out a survey of the membership and asked them to identify their priorities," recalls Chief Frank. "They identified facilities for traditional and cultural activities, education, health services, and tourism. We tried to develop the first three priorities, but we failed because they did not generate enough revenue to pay for themselves. It became clear that cultural activities are not easily commercialized. There was fear, because our value systems are involved, so we stepped back from that."

Chief Frank sees his personal strength as a leader as coming from the elders and the hereditary chiefs. They have taught him to wait and listen until all have spoken so that he knows exactly what he wants to say. Over his five terms, he has taken the opportunity to build a rapport with the community that is a source of strength.

Settlement of the claims will provide his community with more control over their lives. They can develop economic opportunities, grow in
self-esteem, and regain the healthy minds that will ensure that the
claims money is handled properly. The challenge is to encourage people
to train for the positions that will come available, even though the
training process is time consuming and pessimism may set in. Women
are honoured as life givers and are important participants in the community. They make active contributions to the community through
holding elected, hereditary, and administrative positions. They join elders and youth in contributing to developing a healthy future.

In order to map out their traditional lands for the land-claims process
and their own economic development, the Tla-o-qui-aht have a GIS-
mapping project that incorporates cultural information for the use of
members. Dan David is responsible for gathering information from the
few remaining elders and documenting traditional use of areas, the
original names of rivers and mountains, and the history of those
names. He has a strong grounding in this work since he began listening
to the stories of his grandfather and his father when he was a young
boy. Historically the Nuu-chah-nulth were engaged in trade with some
surrounding communities and their relatives in the mainland United
States. It was the women's responsibility to engage in trade.

Education and preservation of the language are the largest challenges
facing the community, according to Dan. Young people have to prepare
for the opportunities in the community that will follow the land-claims
settlement. The language is critical to maintaining culture and tradition.

ENCOURAGING ECONOMIC DEVELOPMENT IN KEEPING WITH THE CULTURE

In the early 1990s, Nuu-chah-nulth Tribal Council set up three councils to
look after the north, south, and central regions in the Nuu-chah-nulth territory. The Central Region Board has a representative from each of five
member communities including Tla-o-qui-aht, Heshquiat, Ahousat, Toquaht, and Ucluelet. The region's hereditary and elected chiefs entered into
negotiations with the federal and provincial governments and concluded
the Interim Measures Agreement, which provided $2 million for economic
development and $500,000 for training for the central region over a three-
year period. An extension was negotiated at the end of the period for an
additional $1.5 million. It was the first such agreement in the province.

A working group was formed to set up the process and make recommendations on suitable proposals. The group has taken a broad mandate and will consider proposals focusing on business, capital projects, and operating fund requirements. Each successful applicant enters into an agreement in which 50 per cent of the award is a grant and 50 per cent is a loan. The loan repayments become the principal of the fund that will continue on for the foreseeable future.

Ann Atleo, a lawyer and member of the Ahousat community, has sat on the working group since its inception. When the fund was established, the working group had two members representing the province. The group now wants the provincial representation removed, Ann says.

They have served their purpose of providing initial guidance and administrative help. They have blocked some applications that the rest of the working group felt should be supported, since they have signing authority before funds are released. The negotiations in these situations take time, and the education about our priorities has to be repeated each time.

For example, the province put a plan in place to downsize the salmon fleet. Several fishermen asked for funding to upgrade or expand their businesses. The provincial representatives took a month and half to sign because they didn't want to be seen by the public as favouring one group.

Another time, a group approached us for funds to improve a building for a very successful preschool program that will benefit kids for many years to come. There was some tension between the provincial representatives who did not support this use of the fund and the Central Region representatives who looked at it from an holistic perspective of benefit to the whole community.

The working group, with three women and two men, has a good balance of life experience, perspective, and formal training (a master's degree and a law degree). Each member is committed to making a difference in the region. Start-up has had its challenges. The group has been criticized for taking too long to consider applications and for requiring too much information. However, their attitude has been that they must be conservative and cautious in favour of supporting a fund that will continue to support economic development initiatives for generations to come. "Members are willing to work and make the extra effort to help things work smoothly," Ann says. "They are supportive of each other and cooperate in improving the living environment generally. Employment is critical, since people want to work and not be on welfare. Young people are furthering their education and coming back to the communities to start their own businesses." She is proud of the way the whole community is supported. A non-native with a band council resolution qualifies to make application to the fund. Working with everyone builds a stronger community.

The working group gives priority to acting professionally and in a timely fashion with applicants in order to maintain good relationships with the communities. They report to the chiefs regularly and ask them to advise their communities about the work of the group. Ann says she finds that people are still unclear about the fund and the work that is being done and so anticipates that in future the group will communicate directly with the community. The working group liaises with the Nuu-chah-nulth Economic Development Corporation and regularly sends applicants to them. They administer federal and provincial economic development programs for the benefit of their whole territory. They work very hard at separating politics and the decisions they take. They have seen a positive impact on people through increased jobs and businesses.

The challenge that Ann finds hardest is saying no to poor ideas that need more work. "We are very careful about giving this sort of news," she says. "We talk about it and select the person who is best. able to give the news as gently as possible. We handle our people with humility."

Ann feels that there are no gender issues working to her detriment as part of the working group. However, she is able to understand community members who treat her as a little girl, despite her formal training. Others are put off by the fact that she went to school and they did not. They see her as a "know-it-all." She works at changing those misconceptions. Sometimes she must handle people with attitudes that question her abilities. She deals with them directly and asks them to help her understand the issues at stake. She notes that she has skills in some areas while they have skills in other areas, but her gender does not make her less of a person.

On the whole the program is going well and has been given an important stamp of approval, with the chiefs giving the group direct decision-making authority.

Members of the community have taken advantage of the access to economic development funds. One large project for the community has included seeking title to land where the residential school had been built.

They eventually succeeded and, with their experience in development, decided to build a hotel and conference centre called Tin Wis, which means "calm waters," and overlooks Clayoquot Sound. Its symbol is the thunderbird, which signifies "the protector of all."

After some negative experience with other projects, Chief Frank states that the community's biggest lesson and strength has been to separate business and politics. They approached the hotel project as a money-making venture and sought as board members business people with expertise, irrespective of their heritage. They teamed up with Best Western because of the skills and training that corporation brought to the table and their experience in meeting the needs of families. The goal is to have 100 per cent employment of Tla-o-qui-aht members. However, day-to-day operations at the centre are beyond the influence of chief and council.

This investment was profitable from the beginning and has outstripped the first three-year projections. People are booking two years in advance, Chief Frank says, and a thirty-six room expansion is being contemplated.

"We know our limits in commercializing our culture, through the guidance of our elders," Chief Frank says. "We originally thought we would have our members dancing and singing for the guests. The songs, however, are sacred to certain families, so that wasn't appropriate, especially if tourists wanted to video or tape-record the performances. Instead our hotel is unique in celebrating our heritage through promoting local artisans. We are the only First Nations-owned hotel in the Tofino area. We bring a sense of our history, culture and values ... The revenues are taxed by the community through property and hotel taxes that are returned to meet the needs of the community."

The community sacrificed many things to have the funds to build the hotel. For four years they gave up new housing and gymnasium facilities for the youth. Chief and council are now moving to rectify the situation and to express their gratitude to the community for their support.

Another strength that Chief Frank identifies is the consistent attitude among community leaders that they do not know everything. They rely on the elders and other advisors who have expertise and they seek consultation in the community. In the case of the hotel, they did not act arrogantly as owners but instead listened to their advisors.

The village of Tofino is not an easy place to develop projects. Many people are opposed to any new project, seeing it as increased competition. Moses Martin, a councillor, recalls that the Central Region Board boycotted businesses in Tofino for most of the summer ten years ago to counter local protest over the hotel. While the hotel is Tla-o-qui-aht's largest project, they are involved with other activities. A salmon enhancement program is a non-profit project to restore the quality of fish resources in the area. They release 500,000 individual fish annually. The big challenge is to increase the number of fish returning to the area at the end of the four-year life cycle. Moses predicts that this project can benefit other user groups including commercial fishermen and local grocery stores, fuel docks, and piers.

SMALL BUSINESS, TLA-O-QUI-AHT STYLE

Individual entrepreneurs offer services to the community and to tourists. Some ensure that their dollars stay in the community to recirculate and support the community. Several ventures of interest include water taxis, wholesale art, and an arts and crafts retail operation.

John Tom, a former logger and fisherman, has a water taxi business operating from Meares Island. He received some help from the band in securing funding for his boat. He ferries schoolchildren, takes tourists through the islands, and provides taxi and transport services of all kinds. "I've carried movie stars, politicians, and famous people like Robert Kennedy, Jr. We take emergency calls all hours of the night, especially for women in labour, and the guys out partying for the night," he says. John has five family employees and relies on a bookkeeper for his monthly records and an accountant for his annual statements. It is a demanding business, and he has not taken a day off since he started.

"I used to operate the only water taxi, but now the competition has grown," John says. "I have three boats, and maintenance costs are quite high. I tapped into the tourist market and was part of Tofino's community information service. They listed everyone who was a member. It went under, and I sure noticed the difference this past summer. I didn't get the business I could have under the service. I must stay on top of every detail in order to survive. The other thing I have never done is drink, which helps me to look after my business. My kids have their education and the opportunity to contribute to the community. I don't recommend anyone go into this business because it is a lot of hard work."

Eugene Martin is an artist whose work is strongly influenced by his culture. He prefers producing his art to dealing with the marketing and promotion side. The community supports his work through featuring it in Tin Wis, and local galleries also carry it. Eugene's pride in his heritage is underlined by his conviction that his images are gifts from the spirits; he has no control over what he produces. He has found peace with these influences, but because his art is so personal it is difficult to deal with the economics of having to sell them. His work adds to the cultural fabric of the community.

Another member of Tla-o-qui-aht who is involved in the arts is Nona Rundquist, a retail operator since 1986. Her business, located in Chemainus on the east coast of Vancouver Island, is called Sa-Cinn [Hummingbird] Native Enterprise. "Sa-a-a Cinn-n" is the song that calls the hummingbird. If the birds come, it is a good omen. The name was chosen by Nona with the permission of her great uncle Dr George Clutesi. The story of Sa-Cinn is told in the form of a song that originally belonged to her great-uncle's mother, recalls Nona (personal communication, 1998).

Nona's grandmother was an hereditary chief, and Nona's sister has taken up that traditional role. In the traditional way, her mother, Pearl Brown, choreographed a dance to accompany the Sa-Cinn song. This dance consisted of hovering over one spot, then darting about freely. In 1952, Pearl performed the dance for Princess Elizabeth, soon to be Queen Elizabeth II.

Nona promotes the art of First Nations people in her gallery and in an adjoining shop that puts local artists' work on t-shirts. A practical nurse for twenty-seven years, she opened up her business when her health did not allow her to continue in the nursing profession. She was interested in providing fair value to First Nations artists, contrary to the business practices of the day. For a single parent, it was not an easy road. She worked hard to build her business without the help of outside funders, taking extensive training in management and other business courses. Eventually she had eleven staff, with two additional outlets at the Departure Bay ferry terminal and the Sydney information booth on Vancouver Island. With an economic downturn, she later closed these outlets and focused her attention on her two main stores.

Nona's independence is integral to her business philosophy. "I do all this on my own," she says. "My uncle trained us that way. I did try [for funding] and I was turned down all four times – probably because of my mouth. I know I can do it myself and I don't need handouts. There are businesses that start with a lot of government funding. They don't last. I tell people that you have to be willing to give 110 per cent if you want to survive in business."

Some of the challenges come from racism, which Nona addresses directly if possible. Lack of support from her own community is harder to change. She works hard to offer quality goods and hire her own community members when possible. She has big plans and would like to get into manufacturing with one hundred employees. Already she has the factory plans completed, but she is determined to generate funds for it without the help of any agency, so she knows her dream may take a long time to realize.

THE FUTURE

As Tla-o-qui-aht First Nation prepares for the land claims, there are pressures on the leadership, the community, and each individual. Moses wants to set an example:

I want to get the message to my own little family. They have to work for the things that they want, and there are lots of opportunities in our community. I didn't think I needed education when I was growing up, but things are different and now you do need it. It is hard to get this message to the young people. We still have a high drop-out rate. The challenge is to work together, and then we can move ahead in development.

We must work with our hereditary chiefs and advisors. We haven't been as respectful of the land as we could be. We need a realignment with our traditional values for the future.

We must listen to the elders regarding the land. It is important that we become more sustainable in our actions.

Alaskan native people came to share their experiences of the pitfalls of land claims settlements. Overall, according to Chief Frank, the land claims settlement will be of benefit, and these benefits will increase if the community is healthy. The leadership wants to learn from experience and deal with the anticipated problems, he says.

I believe it is going to provide our people with the ability to have more control of our own lives, to develop more economic opportunities, and to make the community feel better about who we are compared to where we are today. Right now we still have high unemployment, with many people in social service programs like welfare. I don't feel good about the suffering my members endure today.

The key to any treaty is with the community, and the only way you help the community is to help the people. Healthy minds are needed in order to be clear about the future. Unhealthy people will increase our social problems and will not know how to manage claims money. The healthy growth of our community is the biggest challenge we are going to have.

The path is not an easy one. In 2000, the Tla-o-qui-aht First Nation had to boycott the Agreement-in-Principle process when the federal government transferred their traditional territory to the province for an airport at Tofino. This action, in their opinion, contradicted the integrity of the process. In the end, however, the land claims settlements will be an enormous opportunity for the community.

Chief Frank is optimistic about the future, because the community's values and history rest with the elders, who cannot be guided by monetary wealth. They are the steady influence in the community. With the help of the elders, then, it is possible to make money without being controlled by it.

6

Fort McPherson–Gwich'in Community, Northwest Territories

The experience of FORT MCPHERSON–GWICH'IN COMMUNITY demonstrates the impact of a land claims settlement on a community. Now with ownership of lands and resources as well as funds for economic development, there is new energy as people define their needs. In this case study they share their collaborative objectives for investing financial resources. The connection to the land is honoured, as are the gifts offered by the elders. The community must still meet the challenges of dysfunction and disease for members and their children.

LIVING WITH THE LAND

While self-government is a term that means many things across Aboriginal communities, many people can still remember when it was a reality in their lives. Johnny Charlie, a Gwich'in elder, recalls, "Back in the early '40s, it was native self-government. The chief says what you do when you hunt. They say when to stop hunting in the spring, when to start trapping in the fall, and they know when the minks are prime. The chief would say, 'Okay, you don't set your trap until about the 10th of November.' You would be told when to pick up your traps, and you had to pick them up right away, because if you waited one week, the chief would find out and be on your back."

Connection to the traditional ways of living with the land have been passed down from parents to children. It is no different in Gwich'in communities like Fort McPherson, Tsiigehtchick (Arctic Red River), Aklavik, and Inuvik, located in the western Arctic. Memories are important and are shared by the elders.

Hannah Alexie's traditional values of the land were taught to her by her parents. "My mom taught me how to make dry meat and do house chores, working with moose skin, caribou skin, and all these things. My dad taught me how to hunt and how to set traps. I liked going hunting and trapping with my dad rather than staying home working with moose skin or sewing."

The roles of men and women in passing on traditional learning are quite different, Hannah says. "Men must be strong in the community for their children's sake, stand up together, go hunting and teach their children how to go trapping and hunting. The women's job is to teach their children how to work with moose skin, caribou skin, how to make dry meat and how to set a tent up, how to set spruce boughs in the tent, what kind of wood to use, how to set rabbit snares and how to set traps."

Mary Teya remembers the close support she received from her parents, grandparents, aunts, and uncles. She spent six years at residential school and went right back on the land when she returned home. "I consider myself very fortunate to have all that," Mary says. "I have good self-esteem because I have both cultures. I am part of both worlds with my life out on the land as an Indian, my culture, and my tradition. I also work at the Department of Health for the government. I feel good about what I'm doing."

Living in the modern world has affected the community in many ways. The connection to the land has changed but still continues. Trappers no longer live on the land extensively; trapping, fishing, and gathering are done on weekends or in the spring for several months. The significance of the land to Gwich'in today, however, is not to be downplayed. Sarah Jerome, a Gwich'in member, explains: "The land is our life. The land is the bank. The land is what we support ourselves on. If you look across Canada and at people in other countries who do not have ownership of their land, who cannot go out and live off the land, they're sort of like ... they're lost."

Chief Joe Charlie, from Fort McPherson, has some formal schooling and has lived on the land as a hunter/trapper. He is sensitive to the tensions many of his community face in maintaining a traditional lifestyle while negotiating in a contemporary world full of technology, and he understands the resulting need for healing:

A lot of our young people are caught in the middle. This is the generation that elders have told to keep [their] traditional lifestyle. Yet on the other hand, modern technology is pulling them in that direction too. Many people like to live on the land, but they can do it only for so long. Then they have to come back into town to have their TVs, have money in their pockets, and drive their vehicles.

They need to have ways to figure out what they really want in life, figure out their goals and how to reach them. We are building a healing lodge to help. This is a perfect example where our people took the initiative to say that our people have a problem. We have to start healing before we can start on our healing path.

The healing lodge was the community's first major investment after a land claims settlement.

The challenge for any leadership is to meet the needs of the community while balancing approaches with traditional ways. What is the Gwich'in way? How do members balance tradition with the contemporary lifestyle?

Chief Joe Charlie admits those are hard questions. "A lot of our tradition, we just go by the basics, the necessity, I guess you could call it. The Gwich'in way is if you're hungry, you go out hunting; if you're tired, you go to sleep; if it's daylight, you wake up. That's the way people are always. They didn't worry about money since money had no value to them. They just go with the four seasons and the way Mother Nature went. That's a pretty hard question to answer, I think."

Mary Teya adds, "The Gwich'in way, for sure, is we're friendly and we share. We always make it our business to get to know people and share."

Chief Joe Charlie speaks from personal exerience on the importance of maintaining ties to the land:

I have the better of both worlds now. I'm the chief of Fort McPherson, I have a computer beside me, I have a phone, I have my own desk, and I'm living in the modern world. But if I didn't want this job, I can most likely go out on the land and feel real good about it and stay out there, because I did it for fifteen years, and that's something I treasure.

I guess I'm a very spiritual person and I always thought, down the road, times are going to get tough. I always said that when I first came off the land, I said I was going to work in the community for just a couple of years, and now I feel that I've seen what I wanted to see in the community, and I don't like it. I truly believe that people who live on the land are the most well-off people.

In the community, you worry about bills and you're controlled by time. You get stressed out on that – like you as a researcher, for example. You have a time schedule for me, and you had a time schedule for the principal of Chief Julius School. You cut her off so you can make time for me. You're always structured around time.

If you're out on the land, then you just go by your instincts. You sleep when you're tired, you eat when you're hungry, and you go when it's daylight. There is nice, clean fresh air and there is no stress, none whatsoever. I think that's the lifestyle I like.

The Gwich'in way is changing. According to Dolly Carmichael, people don't look after each other as much as before. "In the smaller communities, I've noticed that people basically look after themselves. They come to the band when they need help. I don't see people just helping each other as much anymore."

Hannah Alexie has also noticed the Gwich'in way changing, but sees room to be hopeful. "Most of the people are going the white man's way. The role of our culture is slowly drifting away from us – but not that much, 'cause I see most of the people still sticking to their traditional way. Whether they're doing it good or not, I won't say, but it's still there."

Roles of men and women have changed. The influences have come from outside and have often been beyond anyone's control. The decline in the fur trade in the 1970s, for example, had a particularly sharp impact on the community. Sarah Jerome, a school principal, describes the changes that followed:

We went through a transitional period during the 1970s when the whole subsistence economy of the community went to a wage economy. The trapping life style of the trappers was phasing out, and the wage economy was coming in. This is where a lot of women in the community – who had education, time to get the jobs, and who were willing to be trained – got into the wage economy. They gradually became the breadwinners of the community. This left our men in limbo. There was no more trapping to be done, and they didn't have the skills or the education to get into these job situations. They were just stuck.

For a long time Fort McPherson was recognized for the women who were working within the community. We had leadership positions and made decisions because we were the ones working. I know that a lot of the men were not comfortable with that, but they had no choice. They automatically turned to the next thing they could think of, which was drinking. This created a lot of social problems within the community.

It wasn't their fault. Many didn't have the education or skills to get jobs. Some had skills to work with oil companies during the oil boom. They worked

in the Delta Beaufort region in exploration. They were not skilled, but they
made a lot of money in a very short time frame. I remember being afraid and
wondering what were we going to do with these people when the oil boom was
over, but I needn't have worried. We were working towards our land claims at
that time, and some worked on the claim. When the land claims were settled,
we got into trucking and road maintenance, and we could start putting our
men into positions where they were working.

Traditional spirituality was also affected during this period, mostly
from the presence of western religions. This is an issue for those communities who seek to recapture traditional spirituality and add it to the
perspectives that are honoured as they live First Nations government.

After twenty-seven years in the community, the mayor, Piet Van Loon,
sees little if any tradition practised in the community. He explains:

Everybody to some extent spends time on the land, and there are a couple of
dozen people who are full time on the land. They have extended families who
have the tradition of being out on the land. I think the tie to the land hasn't
ever been severed, but it's certainly been stretched tight.

I think the Gwich'in language is far richer and goes far deeper than the sort
of traditional ways that people live now. The way of life has really been En-
glishized and Anglicanized. It's become a mixture of Christian and Scottish
ways. The traditional bush life or the traditional life and culture that people
had here is pretty well erased. I include the old songs, dances, and drums. It
started happening in 1850. The Anglican church is a strong tradition here, and
I think that the majority of people have loyalty to that church.

The process of settling the land claims and implementing them has
challenged the Gwich'in communities. Change is inevitable, but the
change that brought about the land claims was one in which the
Gwich'in participated. Other influences on community life include
changing roles of men and women, technology, religion, spirituality,
the impact of the boom/bust oil industry, lack of education, and dysfunction. Community members have risen to these challenges together
and individually.

LAND CLAIMS IMPACTS

A 1973 court decision was the catalyst for the Canadian government's
agreement to negotiate a land claim agreement with the Dene and the

Métis. This marked the beginning of a twenty-year process that gives the Gwich'in the tools they need for self-government. The deal covers many aspects of their lives, including a $75-million cash settlement over a fifteen-year period and title to 24,000 square kilometres of land in the Mackenzie Delta and the Peel River Basin in the Yukon. As well, a number of boards and organizations were formed. These include the Gwich'in Tribal Council, the Renewable Resource Board, and several community councils.

It is critical that the four Gwich'in communities work together. This is accomplished through the Gwich'in Tribal Council (GTC) made up of a board of directors with members from each community. An annual general assembly, with fair community representation, establishes by-laws and elects the president with two vice-presidents, who supervise the day-to-day affairs of the Gwich'in Tribal Council and meet regularly with the board of directors. At the annual assemblies, reports on the activities of each organization, with audited financial statements, are submitted to the communities for their review.

The GTC has a number of wholly owned subsidiaries that in 1994 included a trust fund, a land corporation that administers Gwich'in-owned lands, a development corporation, a settlement corporation for certain investments, and a Social and Cultural Institute.

Fort McPherson is represented by the Gwicha Gwich'in Council, which works with the GTC. It also has a Gwicha Gwich'in Renewable Resource Council, which works with its counterparts in the other communities and with the Renewable Resource Board (RRB). The RRB has representation from the territory, the federal government, and the Gwich'in, and from the broader community through an independent chair. According to Dolly Carmichael, the RRB have responsibilities for determining harvest quotas: "They're responsible for the trees, plants, fish, animals, berries, and even our moss. They'll consult with the renewable resource councils, and the renewable resource councils will carry out harvest studies and needs assessments. We're going to make sure that the Gwich'in needs are met before we allocate any portion of a quota to another group. We want to ensure that there will be trees and animals for the future. Although a lot of us don't get out on the land very often, we still have our ties there, and to me that's still home."

Within this context of setting the course for a future that maintains ties to the land and meets community needs, the role of community leaders is as critical today as it has ever been.

LEADERSHIP

In Fort McPherson a legacy of solid leadership has seen the Gwich'in through the land claims negotiation and is now seeing them through implementation. Consultation, planning, and limiting the use of outside expertise are seen as important. The Gwich'in have researched the experience of other communities, including Native American ones. Alaska's land claims experience began in 1972, and regular visits are coordinated, with corporations formed by Alaskan native land claims. Gwich'in community strengths are complemented cautiously by outside consultants on a short-term basis. They avoid long-term commitments in favour of using their own members and building in-house expertise.

Leaders and community members have engaged in several planning exercises to define their short-term and long-term objectives and strategies for achieving those objectives. Road mapping, a planning technique introduced to the Gwich'in by facilitator Mike Robinson, gives a cross-section of decision-makers and community members the means to build a strategic plan or map. It is a technique used by Esso Resources Ltd. and such organizations as the Rotary Club and the Arctic Institute of North America at the University of Calgary.

Mike explains that the road-mapping process begins from the perspective of participation:

Ideally, you involve as many people as possible from the organization which is seeking strategic planning. The first order of business is to explain what a vision is and why institutions should have visions. In road mapping, the vision explains where the organization wants to be in five years' time – for example, "In the year 2000, we will be the most successful native organization in Canada with respect to stewarding cash earned as a result of negotiating a comprehensive land claims settlement."

The vision is articulated by the entire group. Generally, smaller groups are formed, and then work is accomplished in roundtable format. Each discusses a personal vision held for the organization, and then it's the job of a roundtable captain to forge a consensus that builds the four, or five, or even six individual expressed visions into one consensus vision.

The roundtable approach aims to facilitate creative thinking while building consensus. It ensures the opportunity for all to state their concerns, present facts, discuss issues, and offer suggestions in the development of a strategic plan. It may be revisited and updated regularly.

In 1994 the Gwich'in focused on the financial strategic plan to ensure the Gwich'in Comprehensive Land Claim Agreement would result in future benefits to their communities. There were sixty delegates, Mike recalls. "We divided the delegates into eight round-tables, and there were eight visions that were offered for general plenary discussion."

The Gwich'in Financial Road Map* notes the benefits of community participation. These include promoting ownership of the plan by the community, focusing on specific community needs identified by members, ensuring that benefits will flow to communities, and encouraging empowerment, capacity-building, and consciousness-raising for participants (2).

Out of the collective process, a vision for the year 2000 emerged. Four programs were identified as worthy of implementation: protection and enhancement of the land claims principal; preservation of Gwich'in culture; development of an investment program while promoting education and training for Gwich'in members; and improvement of local education and social systems (4). Once a vision was determined, beliefs and values that are the foundation of the community's spiritual and cultural aspects were articulated.

Values and beliefs with a cultural orientation included: trust, honesty, sharing (like sharing caribou), not mixing politics and business, responsibility, balance, faith in the leadership, religion/spirituality/healing, independence motivation, cooperation, compromising, and continuous improvement. Values and beliefs with a business and human-capital investment orientation included: good judgment and common sense, control and monitoring of investments, reinvestment in the local economy, security of investments, developing long and short-term plans, being risk averse, ensuring well-being and financial stability for future generations, providing money for education, not paying dividends until a healthy rate of return is attained, inflation-proofing the principal, supporting entrepreneurs financially, and encouraging beneficiaries to participate fully in the Gwich'in Development Corporation (5).

These beliefs and values are translated into decisions and behaviour through principles. The Gwich'in describe their principles (7) as follows:

---

* Gwichin Financial Road Map, developed by the delegates at the Gwich'in Financial Roundtable, 17–20 February 1994, Whitehorse, Yukon, Arctic Institute of North America: University of Calgary.

We will:

- conduct business in a professional manner (get all the facts straight);
- work to make safe investments;
- carefully monitor our investments;
- encourage equal participation from all age groups in the community;
- consult with Gwich'in band members;
- provide cooperation and security to our beneficiaries;
- be trustworthy;
- stick to our goals;
- do our research;
- get second opinions;
- have professional work and business plans;
- implement plans once they are complete;
- jump in with both feet when we know that it is time to act;
- leave business to the businessmen and politics to the politicians;
- conduct our business in an ethical manner;
- have quarterly (in house) financial statements available to our beneficiaries;
- provide training and jobs for the Gwich'in and work towards 100% Gwich'in run businesses by the year 2000;
- not take on *very* high financial risks;
- have knowledgeable and enthusiastic management;
- never forget the needs of the community;
- ensure that sharing, learning, trust, honesty and respect are values that are practised when conducting our business;
- maintain and practice open communication and disclose financial information to all Gwich'in beneficiaries to keep them informed and up to date on financial matters; and
- ensure all investment decisions are to the benefit of Gwich'in beneficiaries (7).

The final step in the process was to identify strategies for attaining the four programs (or objectives) that the Gwich'in had identified in their vision for their community. These strategies identified tasks and a time frame for accomplishing the tasks, naming an individual or group to be responsible for developing the strategy, and setting a budget for accomplishing the strategy.

The first objective was to develop a program to protect, maintain, and enhance the land claim settlement. Over a ten-year time frame, they want to select investment managers on the basis of three proposals; undertake a regular review of investment management; give thought to where money should be put, since it is taxable in the Gwich'in Development Corporation (GDC) but non-taxable in the settlement corporations; provide information to beneficiaries; regularly report financial audits to the beneficiaries; review bylaws that protect money; review ways to inflation-proof the principal; distribute interest, assess the pros and cons of dividends to beneficiaries; and allocate a percentage to go to the GDC.

The investment mix was also determined. High-risk investments will make up 10 per cent of their investment portfolio and will focus on business development. Business development projects with moderate risk will make up 20 per cent of their investments. Low-risk business development with government guarantees will make up 20 per cent. The remaining 50 per cent will be placed in a trust fund with low-risk investments.

These plans have since been reviewed and revised by the community. This road map records community priorities when the means to self-government is within their grasp. It demonstrates a process that aids community consensus in which dissenting opinions are heard and decisions taken after hearing all arguments. Values and traditions are inherent in the process – including the tradition of stewarding the environment in a thoughtful manner. Many plans gather dust on shelves for varying reasons, but this process minimizes the possibility that this will happen. Participants have a vested interest in the plan being followed and will remind leaders of this interest.

Different community needs have become priorities for leaders. Healing is a critical need because the fallout from alcoholism and drug abuse, for example, reverberates at all levels of the community, from the children who do poorly in school to the missed job opportunities in the community. The first major investment approved by the community after the settlement was a healing camp funded by land claims money. The government involvement was limited to redirecting program dollars for the same problems into this healing lodge. The lodge would have allowed people to get treatment while being on the land with their families. Unfortunately, the lodge closed because of a failure to find matching grants.

It is hard, but people seem ready for a healing change. Plans for cultural immersion programs for children will be incorporated into new programs. James Ross, a former chief, made his stand by hiring only people who are not drinking. The message is that you have to sober up if you want to work for the band. The school has also followed this policy. The result is that while the community supports the selling of alcohol, opportunities are limited for people who are abusing it. These policies set the stage for building capacity of members who will participate in initiatives requiring skilled people who are sober.

Sarah Jerome, the former school principal, is impressed with this policy. "I really admire our leaders because they have done so much with our money," she says. "They could have paid out money to the beneficiaries. Instead ... they realized that we have to heal. We have to heal our communities, we have to heal our people. We cannot heal one person out of every community, it has to be a family effort."

Willard Hagen, GTC president, has clear ideas of policies he supports including accountability issues. While the community is not under the provisions of the Indian Act, leaders are still limited to a two-year term. Some communities are changing that to a longer period in an effort to give their leaders better opportunities to accomplish their plans. However, Willard supports the two-year term for several reasons:

Leadership does not become entrenched with a short term. I like the two-year term because I think it makes people more honest at the start, and I think it means that they have to work night and day if they want to get credibility and keep it. Continuity of leadership is very, very important, but not if it means someone can pull a con-artist job on the communities. If you can't do it in two years and you argue that you need four years, well then, maybe you can't do it. I said I'd have the claim in two years, and here eight months later we have it. We outdid ourselves. I have a good crew working for me. Robert Alexie Jr's an excellent guy, and James Ross is a very solid leader and a very honest man.

Another way to encourage depth in leadership is to allow people to develop their own skills. Willard is very active, but he pulls back, consciously allowing the people he works with to realize their own skills. He shares some thoughts on the independence resulting from the settlement:

We're taking total control of the organization. Someday soon the government will wake up, realize this has happened, [but] it's almost going to be too late. Our own chairmen are in control of all the boards, which I don't think is going to happen again. We should be in control of all our boards anyway, and when industry comes in, while we're not pro-development, we want balance. Development has to address what's environmentally safe, what's good for the people, what's good for tradition, how many job opportunities are there, how much money's going to stay in our region, and how much control we are going to have over the development. We'll control any development, like a pipeline. We'll build it and lease it back to the government. We'll joint-venture with the Japanese.

Mike Robinson has had dealings with many Aboriginal communities over the years as a consultant and is well informed about strong communities. He speaks very positively about the Gwich'in experience:

I think the Gwich'in are in some ways remarkable and unique, in that they have a tremendous depth of leadership talent. They have youth, young adults, middle-aged folk who carry most of the burden sometimes, and they have elders, all of whom play a leadership role. All integrate well across the age ranges in the communities and care deeply about the future of the Gwich'in language and the Gwich'in people and the Porcupine caribou.

The Gwich'in have, perhaps because of their homeland being distant from the centres of Yellowknife and Whitehorse and Ottawa, avoided to some degree the colonial imprint that communities that are closer to government have received. So there's a Gwich'in sense of purpose, pride of place, and strength of focus that is very strong.

When I'm with the Gwich'in or participating in Gwich'in projects, they are an equal partner. In that sense, there doesn't seem to be a strong legacy of paternal, colonial regimes from government or the church. Another major Gwich'in asset is that a number of the leadership and others have completed advanced education away from the Gwich'in communities and then returned home. There is a formal educational base there that many communities don't yet have the opportunity to rely upon. They have a strong commitment to bright young students completing their education and bringing it back home.

Since the land claim was settled, the best and the brightest of the Gwich'in aspired to be well-employed at home, in the Gwich'in homelands. I don't get the sense that they want to become deputy ministers or ministers or MPs. I think that they would view the best achievement as the achievement that really betters the lives of Gwich'in directly. So there hasn't been a conspicuous loss of Gwich'in talent to other job centres and other sectors.

Another contributory factor, I'm sure, was the early Gwich'in involvement in the '70s and '80s with the oil patch activity in the Beaufort and the Mackenzie Valley. It certainly had its negative aspects in terms of what was very easy, big money, and the opportunity that brought all kinds of material goods and chances to travel and party. The bottom line is that the exposure to that era gave people a chance to see what big money was, what you could buy

with it, and the problems that came with it. It obviously disappeared quickly
if you didn't think about it, bank it, and invest it carefully. That experience
was important.

LAND CLAIMS INVESTMENT

In their financial road map the communities set their priorities for an
investment strategy that would work for the people. The actual
projects that they invested in, after a portion of their funds were invested in financial markets, targeted local companies that met local
needs. Dolly Carmichael talks about the opportunities for those in the
community of Inuvik:

We have a lot more opportunities here than the other communities. We're on
the highway system and there's potential for lots of highway work. There are
lots of government positions that'll open up through community transfers and
also in our leadership. James Ross is a very strong leader. He looks for opportunities for his people and then he takes the initiative. He gets things going and
gets everybody involved.

Our investments have to have some direct impact for our people. It has to
have some value for our people. It's not a money issue. We try and see how it'll
improve the lives of our people. If the benefits aren't there, then I think we'll
just basically invest in the North. We'll stay within our own regions.

In 1994, commercial construction, property management, and
Gwich'in Geographics, a company that handled land-related research
contracts, were the major investments of the Gwich'in Development
Corporation. The construction company provided employment to local
community members on highway contracts, while two office buildings
were operated in Fort McPherson and Inuvik. Gwich'in Geographics
had contracts with a territorial park and projects with the Social and
Cultural Institute. These projects met the criteria for claims investment
with employment opportunities for local people, taking control of local
economic activity and support for people to work and live in the communities. Gwich'in Development Corporation built the two office
buildings with a large training component. It was expensive, but these
trained people will now be able to provide their skills in other projects.

According to Chief Joe Charlie, some people expected to receive a
pile of cash and never have to work again. He says that these percep-
tions have slowly changed as the land-claims settlement activity fo-

cuses on cautious and careful implementation. "I believe land claims have made people more aware that this is *their* claim. Also, if they want to be a part of it, they had better start working and bettering themselves in order to fit into the organization. Get your education, get your feet on solid ground, or get yourself healed, and then start working forward."

Education is becoming more important to young people as they realize that taking advantage of opportunities requires skills and knowledge. The leadership is investing in businesses for members to run. These include entrepreneurial opportunities for members interested in starting their own businesses. Staff provide advice and support for new business ideas. Settlement funds are available to augment government start-up funds for members with a good business plan.

MAKING A STRONGER COMMUNITY

With the land claims has come a sense that positive changes can make a difference now in the attitudes of community members and families and between communities. Members in the community say they feel hope that elders and youth can work together, Gwich'in culture will survive, families will become healthier, and children will be inspired to further their education.

Mary Teya, the first female band councillor, is pleased that an elders' committee and a youth committee are being set up. The process is slow, but she is very encouraged: "It's not easy to do these things, because they've been all done for us before," she says. "Now it's something new and sometimes very confusing. Many times people don't agree with each other about what they're doing, and it causes conflicts. So the people will have to get really serious about all these things. We just can't sit back and expect things to happen for us. We have to be a part of it."

Families are feeling the pressures of modern culture. Mary is concerned that parents go out to play bingo and leave their kids at home to cook dinner for themselves. The closeness of a healthy family is affected, and the teachings that will help the children to understand their culture are minimal. If this trend is not reversed, their culture is threatened, Mary says:

People should be home with their children at night after they come home from school. They should get a good meal for them and put them to bed, and give them support for their education for the next day. They can check into their homework. Instead, there's too many bingos and card games going on in the community. We have to see that our way of life as Indian people, the way that we were taught, the advice, the encouragement and all that – that has to come back somehow, and we need our elders to do that.

Our elders have to bring back that discipline, that advice and encourage-ment, because our children are going to be led astray. They're not going to care, because Mother wasn't there making sure that they went to bed at the right hour and so for that reason, they get up at a late hour. They miss out on their morning, or they're sleepy or unhappy. Nobody cares, so why should they care? So this has to come back.

The parents and grandparents have to teach the children. If they plan to take them out on the land for weekends and teach and talk to them, it will be good. When you're out on the land, you listen to each other in one room where you eat together and you sleep together. You share your work, and during those times parents can be telling them about their grandparents and how they used to live. They can teach how important it is to share and talk. We don't talk as much now, and people go their separate ways with TV. We have to realize that there are changes that we have to take control over.

This caring has been lost in the community too. In our Gwich'in way, when our young people made mistakes, they didn't just get condemned for it. The el-ders were asked by the parents to speak to them. Whether it was not listening or spousal assault back years ago, chief and council went to whomever was abusing their wife and they talked to the family. They would say, "What you're doing is not right," but they didn't condemn them for it. I'm asking people in the community to bring that caring attitude back.

We have problems in our community. It may be alcohol problems, suicide or problems of abuse – when we see one of our people causing other people prob-lems, we know that it's not right. We should make the effort to go and talk with them before it gets worse. If we see signs of depression or suicide, we should make it our business to talk with them. Don't wait. Don't watch it happen.

With the increased development activity, more opportunities are avail-able for people with some education and training. Education is still rel-atively rare, although the Gwich'in leadership is evidence of the growing trend of getting educated and working in their communities. Many parents and grandparents do not have extensive formal educa-tion and, recalling the pain of residential schools, they are not overly supportive of education for their children. This has created a challenge for those interested in improving the level of education in Gwich'in young people.

Sarah Jerome discusses some of the challenges in education facing the community.

A lot of grandparents take their grandchildren in and try to raise them, but without boundaries. Those are the kids that you have the most problems with, so our first challenge, I think, is to educate the grandparents and the parents to make them realize why education is so important. I think our next challenge is to work with leadership to support us because the next generation has to be educated. They are backing us because they realize that they're not going to be in positions like that forever. We have challenged the leadership and the different organizations within the community to work with us as a team to start pushing the importance of education.

Another challenge our young people have asked for is to teach [them] academics ... plus our bush skills. If we can include those two, then the youth say they'll be knowledgeable on the land and about education. We'll be happy in both worlds, and we'll have a foot in each culture.

An elder said, "You have your knowledge about the Gwich'in culture and the language, and you have your education. You can live anywhere in Canada with the dominant society, so you've got a foot in both cultures, you're superior, because you're right in the middle. I, on the other hand," he said, "am only knowledgeable about the Gwich'in culture and language. I don't know the white man's language and culture, so therefore I'm way over here. The person that's a white person or that was brought up in the white dominant society is over here, so you're right in the middle and you're right up there."

What we have to make the students realize is that they have to have both cultures and be knowledgeable about both.

Non-Gwich'in community members are involved in the local hamlet council. Piet Van Loon, the mayor and a resident of more than twenty-five years, notes that while councillors are not all involved directly in economic development, they are involved in planning for the community. They make sure industrial property is available and that it is serviced. They are involved in zoning and enjoy a positive relationship with chief and council. They share ideas in regular weekly meetings. This positive relationship benefits the whole community.

The land claims required some difficult negotiations with the Gwich'in's neighbours, the Inuvialuit. The Inuvialuit settled their claim in 1984 and as a result took a leadership role in the community of Inuvik. There was some overlap in both claims that had to be worked out.

Dolly Carmichael remarks on how the disputes were resolved and on how the community has drawn together when facing an important issue:

There were a lot of problems working out the overlap agreement. It was more problems with the leadership, because neither would give in. What happened was the community councils just said, "Since you guys can't solve it, then we're taking it away from you, and the communities will decide." They took their power away, let the community decide, and they had an agreement within two weeks.

When we have some common conflict that affects the community as a whole, it really draws everybody together. We just had a big meeting and you saw the Gwich'in, the Inuvialuit, and the non-Natives all grouped together to solve this issue. I think that was a big turning point, because we got involved in other social activities together.

The future is bright for the Gwich'in and their communities. Elder Hannah Alexie thinks the future is good for the children. She does not speak about challenges facing the community. She says that is not the Gwich'in way, and it is the Gwich'in way that means everything.

"I don't think 'challenge' is the right word to use among us Gwich'in people," she says. "We know how to live out on the land. If we see one of us doing something wrong, then we teach them how to do it right so the next time he or she goes out on the land, they can do these things. We teach one another, so that 'challenge' is not the right word. We have to use the word 'sharing.' We're all Gwich'in people here. We share what we experience, we share what we know, we share our culture. That is where our future is."

The Gwich'in land claims process has honed leadership skills and brought opportunities for self-sufficiency. Community members are participating in plans for investment of the settlement funds and in new business. The leadership has clear direction and is focusing on investments that benefit the community and provide employment opportunities. Once these opportunities have been tapped, regional investment opportunities will be investigated. When required, consultants are relied upon for specific, clearly defined tasks.

Relationships within the community and with neighbours have changed as more opportunity exists than ever before. While contemporary society is compelling, many want a blend of both the modern and traditional ways to be available to young people. The Gwich'in way of life must be preserved, and strong families must be nurtured. The dysfunction that exists in the communities will be addressed so that healthy communities can flourish.

PARTNERING
IN DEVELOPMENT

7

Tribal Councils Investment Group, Manitoba

TRIBAL COUNCILS INVESTMENT GROUP represents a unique partnership. Manitoba's tribal councils recognized the need for a vehicle that would make investments beyond their individual capacities. The group took an initial investment of $25,000 from each tribal council and has returned it many times over with annual payments. TCIG's national investments include a Pepsi bottling franchise that is wholly owned and a non-insured health benefits company that is a partnership with a large health insurance company. The group partnered with Aboriginal organizations in Saskatchewan, Northwest Territories, and the Yukon on an investment project in The North West Company.

PARTNERING AMONG ABORIGINAL COMMUNITIES

TCIG is an Aboriginal partnership unlike any other in Canada. In 1990, Manitoba's seven tribal councils came together to form a partnership designed to invest in major projects that were beyond their individual capacities. By the mid '90s, several lucrative investments in companies were earning revenue and generating profits. More than $2 million in profits had been returned on equity and distributed annually to fifty-five Aboriginal communities, representing a total of 92,000 First Nations shareholders. Other investments were being considered and had increased TCIG's balance sheet to the $30 million range.

A TIMELY PARTNERSHIP

This partnership is noteworthy on a number of fronts. Its partnering of seven tribal councils is without historical precedence. For many years, issues of survival have overwhelmed Aboriginal leaders. For most communities, these issues are still pressing, but TCIG has given some breathing space and allowed these communities time to contemplate the means of moving away from dependence on government funding.

Board chair Philip Dorion has been with TCIG since its inception. He recalls its creation:

Some of us were working together, and we were looking to purchase a restaurant. We had made several overtures to people, but somehow the deal fell through. Another project came our way while we were talking about the concept of TCIG, so we were forced to incorporate quickly. The project we were considering had employment potential for our people, and at that time some chiefs supported the idea of TCIG.

We wanted to be in the position to look at opportunities presented by Winnipeg or the province that would make things better for our people. It might be through employment opportunities, or owning a hotel for them to stay in when they come into Winnipeg.

Indian Affairs and the tribal councils financed the operations and office set-up. We said that we would be self-sufficient in three years. Each tribal council put in an initial amount for investment capital. In the first few years we didn't pay dividends to the tribal councils. While we are still a long way from the hotel and other kinds of services that we initially talked about, our first investment allowed us to pay our shareholders each year since then.

Meaningful participation in the local economy was part of the drive behind TCIG. The board consists of one member from each tribal council who is appointed by the tribal council chief each year, a president and CEO, and a vice-president. Marvin Tiller held the original position of president and chief executive officer, and Allan McLeod was vice-president and assistant to the president and CEO. Recently, Allan stepped into the lead position with several new staff.

The mandate of TCIG is to have long-term involvement in the mainstream economy by becoming a significant member of the investment community. Its priorities are employment opportunities, transferring technology to shareholders for economic development, earning a reasonable rate of return, and creating a capital pool (Tribal Councils Investment Group of Manitoba Ltd., 1997, 4). TCIG has been successful in accomplishing many of these elements in its mandate.

Phil Dorion explains that TCIG avoids competing for projects with communities or tribal councils. "When a project comes forward for consideration by the board, then those who have the cash and interest in the project will invest. Sometimes they can all afford it, sometimes they cannot. Our original concept was that if we identified an investment opportunity, then the First Nations located next to the project would have the opportunity to take on the project with our help and advice. That First Nations could decide to refer the project to the tribal council. Then the tribal council might decide to develop it or pass it to TCIG because it is too big."

Marv Tiller continues: "We don't want to interfere with critical opportunities for community development. TCIG focuses on the larger opportunities and recognizes that all community members need to contribute to their own economies."

TCIG has a philosophy and a set of investment criteria that allow it to take roles at the local, regional, and national level (10). These include, in particular,

• TCIG does not compete with First Nations communities, economic development groups, or tribal councils.
• Our policy is to only get involved in projects beyond the capacity of an individual group.
• When projects of a local or regional nature come to our attention, we automatically forward the information to the appropriate group.
• The local group may pursue the interest solo, request us to partner with them, request our advice on the project, or pass on the opportunity.
• TCIG also accommodates independent bands and private investors in its investment activities.

In inviting Marv to assume the position of president and CEO, the board knew that he would open the door to mainstream business. Through his background as president and CEO of The North West Company and vice-president and general manager of Hudson's Bay Company's Northern Stores, he has cultivated extensive business contacts in Manitoba and Canada. He is comfortable and familiar with the world of high finance and with managing large investment projects. He is conservative in his approach to investments and absolutely committed to success for TCIG's shareholders.

His sensitivity to the issues of First Nations comes from spending years in First Nations communities all across the country, Marv says. "I watched and became very interested. The first time I was approached for this position, I said no, but when I listened to what they were actually trying to do, I thought that this was really interesting." First Nations communities are getting involved in the economy and generating some wealth through TCIG. This is the ultimate push to self-government or at least to a decent standard of living and a decent level of participation in the community by generating wealth."

In 1993, TCIG approached the Canadian Council for Aboriginal Business (CCAB) to locate an Aboriginal person to bring into the company. The goal was to have Marv train someone to eventually take over as president. Allan McLeod, a member of Cross Lake First Nations, was then a third-year medical student at the University of Manitoba. He had begun to re-examine his attraction to medicine and had found he was more interested in business. When he approached CCAB to discuss the possibility of working with a business person, he was paired with TCIG. Allan worked his way from management trainee to project manager and then to vice-president in six years.

Allan brings to TCIG an understanding of how the Aboriginal community works. He is able to provide insight into board process that is not immediately clear to Marv. The two men formed a strong team, each bringing to it complementary strengths. Allan observes that Marv's appointment was critical in beginning to build credibility: "I think the original board have to be commended for going out into industry and finding a senior executive like Marv. He has a tremendous track record over a number of years in the business. It is his business experience and contacts that enabled us to close the Pepsi deal."

Both are accepted members of the business community. They bring their contacts from other board memberships to bear on TCIG's business whenever possible. Most major Manitoba deals that are in the making will come across their desks. Their process of screening deals and putting them together is discussed in the next section.

INVESTMENT PROCESS
AND CURRENT INVESTMENTS

Under Marv's and Allan's leadership, TCIG has earned an excellent rate of return for its shareholders and paid the tribal council teams a management fee for all their extra services. In 1997 and 1998, TCIG was listed in the top one hundred Manitoba companies. Its rate of return is important, but TCIG is also linked strongly to the concerns of the shareholders. Job opportunities are important, but the company also hopes to give significant amounts of money to each tribal council for the benefit of their communities beyond their government funding.

TCIG takes a cautious and conservative approach to investments, which tend to be in the services sector. These include food and beverages, transportation, data processing, health care, and financial services. Joint ventures are considered with knowledgeable partners in projects in which TCIG can assume a significant ownership position including board membership. Board influence allows TCIG a way of influencing policy, strategy, plans, and outcomes (11) in these investments.

The company stays away from higher-risk startups, turnarounds, and bankruptcies. It uses the resources necessary to hire experts in its due-diligence process in assessing the risk and return of potential investments. Surprisingly, says Marv, TCIG has learned that there is no amount of money too small to pull together at the outset and do something significant with: "We learned we just have to develop a spirit of doing the project right and then levering it."

In the early years TCIG became a founding shareholder in Spaceport Canada, a project to develop the world's first international, commercial, polar rocket launch site at Churchill, Manitoba (18). The project has potential but is presently on hold.

In 1991, TCIG purchased Arctic Beverages, a soft-drink bottling plant, from a family with a small distribution network in Manitoba and a short distance into Saskatchewan. The fifty-year-old company was a going concern, with a history of profit and an opportunity for growth, Marv recalls. "It was not just distributing Pepsi soft drinks but it was distributing juice, water, and other similar products. It was the kind of a company that would generate a cash flow that would allow us to meet our objective of financial independence."

However, Pepsi Cola had to agree to the transfer of the franchise. "Their reaction was long and deep and hard," says Marv: "'why would we sell a Pepsi Cola franchise to a bunch of Indians from Manitoba?' Well, we put together a pretty impressive business plan, and we formed an alliance with the president of the Pepsi Cola franchise on the West Coast. It was approved here and in New York. Today they are very proud of this franchise, since it is the only Aboriginal-owned franchise worldwide."

Since then, TCIG has expanded distribution east into Ontario, west to the Alberta border, and north throughout the Territories. It distributes its product out of its Flin Flon plant to outlets in Toronto, Montreal, Winnipeg, and Edmonton and to three outlets in Manitoba. In 1995 it was nominated for the International Pepsi Bottling Company of the Year Award and placed second overall in Canada and fourth overall in North America (15). It was named as the fastest-growing Pepsi franchise in North America in 1998. This is a noteworthy accomplishment, given that less than 20 per cent of the Canadian population is located north of 60°.

Marv describes the active role that the board has taken in promoting Arctic Beverages products through the "tribal council team." They spend "all kinds of time promoting the products and preaching the gospel of ownership at every powwow, Indian days, golf tournament and hockey game. They do great work."

In 1997, TCIG formed the First Canadian Health Management Corporation in partnership with Aetna Health, a subsidiary of a billion-dollar multinational company. The corporation successfully bid on a government contract to administer the non-insured health benefits program for Canadian Aboriginal people. The five-year contract, with two, two-year renewals, processes annual claims of $300 million. It employs forty-five people, 60 per cent of them Aboriginal. The contractual obligation of one-third Aboriginal employment is a condition that TCIG is pleased to meet and exceed. The contract fell under the Procurement Strategy for Aboriginal Business (PSAB) and is administered by the federal government to encourage more Aboriginal businesses in contracting with the federal government to supply 3 per cent of its $14 billion goods and services.

NAILING DOWN THE CHALLENGES
AND REASONS FOR SUCCESS

Inder Roopra, a TCIG board member and the Southeast Tribal Council's director of finance, is pleased with TCIG's performance. He sees it as providing the opportunity for Aboriginal communities to get involved in big projects – the next logical step after their years of experience with small projects. But he recalls that there was initial trepidation on the part of community members when the idea of TCIG was first proposed:

People were nervous about getting into business, when we talked about it at the community and board levels. Some predicted that it was not going to be successful. Mainly they were afraid of something new. They said that the number of Aboriginal people is too small, and we really can't compete in these businesses. My reply was that you don't have to have big numbers but you have to think big. I use the Jewish people as an example of people who have been very successful in this country, mainly because they think big. Aboriginal people can be successful on the same basis.

Southeast Tribal Council has been very supportive of TCIG. Generally, however, I believe that Aboriginal people are their own worst enemies. One of the biggest problems is jealousy. People do not accept other successful Aboriginal people. Now that TCIG is successfully paying dividends to shareholders through some investments, we have to balance the need to continue growing with those who want a quick return or want to pay dividends before the business is viable.

This is an ongoing educational process. Currently TCIG's board consists of two or three directors who are chiefs, and others who are economic development officers, and those with finance backgrounds. It gives a good balance, but there is some turnover about every two years. This requires that new board members be educated. There is always the pressure from the politicians for more dividends to the shareholders until they understand that a good business needs to grow five or ten years before paying dividends. In about a year's time most of TCIG's debt will be repaid, and that money can be used to invest in other projects in Manitoba.

TCIG has a number of criteria for making investment decisions that balance financial with community needs. According to Inder, buying Arctic Beverages was a "business decision that made economic sense. The numbers looked good. With the insurance company, it helped to be Aboriginal [to qualify for the government's procurement strategy], mainly because we had no experience in insurance. But we took a partner, Aetna Insurance, that strengthened our bid. It is a deal that really focuses on Aboriginal people, but it was a business decision."

It is important that community members understand TCIG and its investments. This is a task undertaken by each of the tribal councils. Some, like Southeast, issue annual reports that include a a description of TCIG's activities. People do not always read the literature nor understand its impact, Inder admits. But Southeast Tribal Council encourages their members to purchase Pepsi and support their ownership.

Joe Malcolm, the executive director of SE Tribal Council, says that when TCIG was formed, he fully supported the philosophy behind it. "I believe in what the people are trying to do. We are helping our own First Nations in the province get into business partnerships with non-Aboriginal people. That is the way to go. I think it is time that we as Aboriginal people take over, and I am a firm believer in TCIG as a good vehicle for very, very successful investments."

Partnerships work well for TCIG. They had no experience with insurance until they became involved with their partner, Aetna Insurance. Through partnerships they are able to bring in the expertise that they lack. Marv sets out what needs to be in place for successful partnerships: "A proper partner is one that you have checked out and trust. TCIG is always a serious partner who participates on the board of directors. Other partnerships are necessary to get things done. You need to recognize financial banks as capital partners, and you need municipal, provincial, and federal government partners. You have to get these people working to your advantage on lucrative opportunities."

In Marv's opinion, people from all walks of life believe that now is the time to form partnerships with Aboriginal people, to push the Aboriginal situation towards making a positive contribution to the economy. Allan agrees, and he stresses how important the process of building relationships is for their business:

We identify groups that are successful, and it's not always money. We've done deals where they have had the same attitude and motivation as us. That is critical. We've had groups with $100 million on their balance sheet with land claims money and all kinds of great things, but these groups will have someone in charge who is suspicious in nature and not very friendly. In terms of our due diligence and looking at partners, we don't care about their money if they have this baggage and don't have the ability to trust. We say, "No deal."

The process is meeting, greeting, interviewing, and it is all a matter of trust and relationships. If we're comfortable with them, then we can do deals. We can now do deals in all of Saskatchewan because there are couple of key guys there we share the same beliefs and values with.

Minimizing politics in board operations has contributed to TCIG's success. Phil recalls that some chiefs who came to early TCIG meetings became bored with the mundane business discussions and are now comfortable leaving it in the hands of board members. Chiefs appoint the TCIG board members and tend to appoint people who have some business experience; often these are the executive directors of the tribal councils. There are also chiefs on the board whose immediate concerns, influenced by their short terms in office, must be balanced with the long-term objectives of TCIG.

Balancing competing interests is not easy. Marv describes how a retreat for all the board members and other invited guests helped them stay on track: "We did that in an effort to validate the direction of what we are doing and what we are not doing. We wanted to identify changes or modifications. It started out pretty tense but it was almost a love-in at the end of the second day. One senior person who was not on the board said that this is not an organization for politicians: let the politicians operate in the political venues, and keep the business here. We have gone a certain distance and it would be a shame to stop. A lot of the politicians recognize that as well. They tell us that TCIG is their company and we are doing a very good job of managing it. [They say,] 'Let us know when you need political help and our support.'"

As chairman of the board Phil Dorion has good relationships with TCIG's president and directors. He is comfortable in his role and often is able to deal with directors directly to sort out any problems.

Protecting TCIG's credibility with the Aboriginal and non-Aboriginal communities is critical to ongoing success. Marv and Allan do not want it to be viewed as another Aboriginal company that failed. TCIG takes pains to adhere to high standards of best business practices to ensure credibility and effectiveness, Marv says:

The best practices in business are followed by many companies, and we have to keep those same best practices. Due diligence on potential investments is important. It is important to go in with an open mind, without preconceived ideas, and no political agenda. We let the financial analysis evolve and take us where it takes us. If it is a bad deal, then we say it. "No deal" is better than a bad deal.

Accountability to our board and shareholders is critical. It is part of good government, so it shows in many ways. We are very fussy about accounting and having proper rules and regulations for spending and harvesting our shareholders' money. It is important for the peace of mind of the shareholders and the survival of any company. These rules maximize good government and minimize conflicts of interest.

Other rules help. We have not had any problems of nepotism because our board is so committed to best practices. We try to find the best people for our operation. They have got to meet the standards and do the job. If you cannot meet standards, then you should not be here, or you should get yourself prepared so you can.

Another example is how we handle cheques. We report to the board on all the cheques that are written. Our vice-chairman co-signs all cheques. Twice a month we list the cheques for him that we propose writing and get his okay. He says no when he is uncomfortable so it is a protection issue. All of this activity is reported to the board once a month.

The leadership vision for TCIG is a long-term one. Marv stresses the importance of keeping this perspective in the minds of community members and newcomers unfamiliar with the company's goals. It's like the goose that lays the golden eggs, he says: "It kicks out a golden egg every year. Some might want to kill the goose now and dig out the last seven eggs. We urge everyone to consider what will happen if we just nurture the goose and let it grow its family. Soon we will have one hundred golden geese giving an egg each per year, which is a lot better than just seven now."

This long-term vision applies to employment of Aboriginal people in key TCIG positions. It takes time for educated people to acquire the expertise and industry experience that is required in the managerial positions. The foundation is being laid right now, and more opportunities are becoming available to build a pool of talent. This talent will be ready to assume leadership roles in the future.

GROOMING THE NEXT GENERATION

Another significant plan for TCIG is that Allan will eventually take up the presidency. This is an outstanding opportunity on a personal level, but it is also an extraordinary signal to other young Aboriginal people. Allan is breaking trail for the next generation of Aboriginal business people.

Allan is cognizant of his value as a role model to Aboriginal youth. He carries an Aboriginal Youth Achievement award with pride. He takes in stride the learning required for the position he is being groomed for and is grateful for the opportunity and the experience. He wants the best for his family and his community and is willing to put in long hours apprenticing with Marv.

Allan spent his early years in Cross Lake, Manitoba, where he travelled to school by boat. When his family moved to Winnipeg, he was the only Aboriginal student in his new school. This did not bother him as he was proud of his Aboriginal heritage. He excelled in sports and was elected class president each year. In his senior years, however, he began to lose a grip on that pride. He looked to name brand jeans and sunglasses for validation of his worth and to make him feel better inside. When he was eighteen years old, he was invited to attend several workshops that strengthened his shaken identify:

I took a program called "Discovering the Power Within" and another called "Flying on Your Own." What I picked up was that it doesn't matter what happens out there, if I change me and how I interpret the world, then I can still be happy. That has been the most valuable lesson I have received to date. I'm comfortable in new situations in the business world and have been successful because I have that tool.

These programs came out of Alkali Lake, B.C., where they had a 95 per cent alcoholism rate and moved to a 95 per cent sobriety rate within ten years. I also learned about maintenance. If you have a lawn during summertime and it is full of dandelions, the program taught us those dandelions represent issues. The program was like a lawnmower that cuts everything down and makes it look nice. In a week the dandelions are back with the nice hot weather, so it's a constant process of always going back there. I credit that for being able to see, feel, and touch what it is like to live with a lawn without dandelions.

The next step in my growth was to examine the root cause of all of these issues. I had to pull the roots out of the dandelions so that they don't grow back. If one or two grow back, it doesn't take much energy to go and pick them out. I got rid of the baggage that would lead to failure.

With this training, Allan was able to accept the internship offer with TCIG. He has a lot to learn, but after eight years he is very comfortable in his position. When he first accepted the internship, it was to be for three to six months. He believes that he will continue to learn for several more years before taking on the position as president. He recalls that at the beginning he was almost ready to pack it in:

My first six months were rough. We were moving to the Commodity Exchange Tower, and I didn't know where it was. I walked in, and the gold elevator doors closed. At some point during that first six months I said, "I don't belong here," and I began to question whether I should stay. What really helped was a conference I went to in Toronto with my mentor, Marv.

When I saw Bay Street, the wealth, and the Royal Bank building with real gold in the windows, I thought, "This is where you make big money." It was a turning point that helped me when I came back to Winnipeg. I thought, "This was nothing but bush league." This helped me get over the gold doors. I now knew that there was something bigger and better out there. This was really just a stepping stone, and something I could handle.

Another important aspect of Allan's life that gives him strength is his culture. After the Alkali Lake training, he began to reclaim that culture. He participated in sweat-lodge ceremonies where he received the spiritual training he had dismissed when he was growing up. Back then, it had made him feel ashamed, Allan recalls:

It wasn't okay until I was okay with myself and I was okay with being Aboriginal and understanding more clearly what our culture has to offer. I have my Indian name now, and I was presented with a pipe before I was married five years ago. There was a feather on the top of the stem. After my Alkali Lake training, I would always talk about the feather. There is one path down the middle, and there are these side paths. I shared what I learned – there are many paths to get off the right road. Others told me that there are many short ones, and you can easily get back on the right track and they are all interconnected. They have been great teachings for me. It was truly amazing that the pipe I was presented with had that feather.

What my culture has really done is allowed me to be comfortable with who I am and what it means in the real world, what the teachings have to offer. I have been able to use them in the business world. I respect people, and it may be a dog-eat-dog world but if you carry yourself with dignity and respect and you can treat others like that, then they in turn will treat you that way. It has really allowed me to be totally comfortable with who I am, have a clear mind, and know that what I have to do for my family in the other world of business is to bring balance and harmony.

Allan wishes now that he had earned his master's degree in business administration early on in his education career in conjunction with his personal healing. His personal healing gives him his emotional intelligence – a positive attitude and motivation. He also likes to share the following story with young people at every opportunity:

Somewhere along the line, I don't know when it happened, I started having these limiting beliefs – I can't do this, Natives can't do that, I could never make money, money is evil – all kinds of limiting beliefs. Out of my Alkali Lake training, they said, "Allan, just remember your community is like this bucket of crabs and what you've learned here is that you're in this bucket and you're going to try to get out. One will climb on another and get his hook over the edge, attempting to pull himself out, and another will come and grab him by the tail and pull him back in. You'll never get out, and remember that is how your communities are." I believed that for a while.

A non-Aboriginal person told me another more appropriate story as to what's really going on with our communities. He said, "Do you know how to train these little fleas to stay in that coffee cup? These things can jump many hundreds of times their body length, from here to the wall or ceiling. Tons of potential. For us to jump one or two body lengths, you have to have big legs. You can train these fleas to stay in a cup. You gather them up and put them in the cup and cover them up. What you'll hear is the rat-tat-tat-tat, and that's them jumping. It hurts, because every time they jump they hit their heads and they fall down. After a while they will settle down and they will start walking around the bottom again. You get them all excited by shaking them up. Rat-tat-tat, and you go through this process for a period time until when you shake them up, you won't hear anything.

At that point they are trained. They are smart and know that if they jump too high, they hit their head, they hurt and they fall down. Now they only jump to the rim. It is comfortable there, no pain. Now you can take the lid off and try to let them go. They won't leave. They have taken the physical barrier and internalized it into a limiting belief. No one else can see it or understand it. Then you get a flea who has broken this belief, but the other ones still won't come along.

That's a good analogy for what's happened to us as Aboriginal people. We're this cup of fleas, and we say, "If only we had more schools, money, or jobs, it would be better." It reminds me of my own experience of "If only the outside world was different, then I would be better." It's not until we can get past our own limiting beliefs and say, "It doesn't matter – what is important is that I feel great about myself and can reclaim my personal power and abilities to start jumping out of the cup and using the potential we all have." I've been able to go into the past and see who I am and clear out all the root causes of all of these issues. Now I am out here where there are tons of opportunities for kids.

THE FUTURE

The future is bright for TCIG. A partnership with Saskatchewan and Northwest Territory groups recently marked a new page in building partnerships with other Aboriginal groups. TCIG took a leadership role in forming Rupertsland Holdings Inc., a consortium of western-based Aboriginal groups. They purchased 450,000 units in The North West Company, a northern-based retail operation that has done business with Aboriginal people for hundreds of years.

This purchase makes them one of the largest shareholders in the company. Keith Martell, chairman of Rupertsland Holdings, noted in the *Winnipeg Free Press* (15 July 2000), "First and foremost, this is a good investment ... The company has a long history of good earnings, good dividend yields, and its stores are an integral part of many First Nations communities. This investment also represents the next step in aboriginal self-determination ... This represents some control of our economic future. We'll now have something to say about where it's going." Such partnerships with other Aboriginal groups will breed opportunities to share the wealth and expertise and ensuing benefits for Aboriginal peoples.

Allan is optimistic about all the opportunities to partner as he meets more people interested in doing business. "I have a running joke that our guys have a lot of bullet holes in their shoes because they shoot themselves in the foot and the deal falls apart," he says. "I don't mean it in a derogatory sense, but it is just my interpretation of what goes on. We tend to fight over the profit before we nurture the business and allow it to grow and build. I would rather have a percentage of a growing, healthy business than 100 per cent of a negative, no-win deal type of company. The more people we get in senior positions where we can trust them, who are confident in who they are and what they can do, the more limitless the possibilities."

TCIG promises to be a source of income beyond what the government gives to Aboriginal communities. Taxation issues will have to be addressed; TCIG's profits directly benefit Aboriginal people, so they should be exempt from taxation in the same ways that municipalities, provinces, and crown corporations are exempt. In any event, Inder predicts that TCIG will be ten times bigger in ten years, owning services such as airlines, hotels, and health services. "Someone with a prescription in a remote northern community might call TCIG, who would deliver it from our pharmacy on our airlines," he says.

In conclusion, TCIG is an outstanding example of an Aboriginal-owned company making a difference in the mainstream economy. It operates with a clear vision shared by its board of directors, who represent approximately 75 per cent of Aboriginal people in Manitoba. The philosophy is driven by business and shareholder objectives. It balances political pressures with "best practices" business principles. Dividends from activities flow to the communities and ensure their needs are met, including their own Aboriginal cultural goals.

The management team utilizes its expertise to capitalize on opportunities in the mainstream economy and within Aboriginal communities. Marv's expertise and his connection to the non-Aboriginal business world balances Allan's insight into the Aboriginal community. The mentorship aspect of their relationship is building a solid foundation for TCIG's continued success. Bringing young leaders into positions of readiness characterizes the strategies of many successful businesses, but as yet there are not as many examples as there could be in Aboriginal communities and organizations.

TCIG's attitude is to act respectfully, with integrity, and to build credibility as reliable business partners. Marv enjoys developing relationships with new people and working in a company with steady positive growth. Allan is thrilled to watch an Aboriginal company's fast growth and to have the opportunity to work with top business leaders. He is taking an active role in decisions that will affect future generations of Aboriginal children.

Current investments are providing solid cash flows and employment opportunities. They are also facilitating the government's responsibility for health needs of First Nations people. TCIG is reaching out to Aboriginal groups and forging new partnerships that will benefit Aboriginal people beyond Manitoba. The Manitoba First Nations community is enriched in many ways by TCIG's existence.

8

Bigstone Cree Nation, Alberta, and Alberta Pacific Forest Industries

BIGSTONE CREE NATION have a number of resources that the community is interested in developing and have entered into a memorandum of understanding with Alberta Pacific Forest Industries, Inc. (Al Pac). Initially Bigstone resisted speaking to Al Pac since they were more interested in protecting their forests from exploitation. Over time, their concerns have changed, resulting in the signing of the agreement.

Al Pac was formed to develop the forestry management area in the vicinity of a number of communities including Bigstone. The company's initiative to understand and work with the Aboriginal communities in their area is unprecedented in the industry. Aboriginal communities are able to demand benefits they have never before received. Employment and business opportunities are the main areas in which these partners work. It is not an easy process, but it is well worth it.

Bigstone is also interested in developing its oil and gas resources. As well, the community has opened a pharmacy.

A COMMUNITY ON THE MOVE

Building partnerships is a demanding process, but understanding the desires and needs of the other side makes success more likely. How does a corporation in a mainstream industry understand the needs of Aboriginal communities? More and more companies are dealing with this question, some better than others. The question of how to build understanding is being asked by Aboriginal leadership too. Understanding those at the table leads to better decisions. Understanding how far industry may go towards working effectively with their communities helps Aboriginal leadership build strong strategies that can help make positive differences.

Bigstone Cree Nation in northern Alberta is dealing with resource companies wanting to do business with them. They are located in the forestry management area (FMA) of Alberta Pacific Forest Industries, or Al Pac. Al Pac entered into a memorandum of agreement with Bigstone as one of a number of initiatives to work with Aboriginal communities in their FMA. What are the opportunities and challenges facing Bigstone? How can they work successfully with Al Pac and other resource industries while still protecting the environment? The environmental impact assessment review process points to Al Pac's need to work closely with local communities. How is this goal being translated into an action plan? These questions are examined in the following sections.

UNDERSTANDING BIGSTONE CREE NATION

Bigstone Cree Nation encompasses seven distinct areas of land. The five main areas are known as Wabasca, with some of the land bordering on the shores of Wabasca Lake and Slave Lake. According to Indian Affairs statistics, Bigstone has 5,500 registered members with more than 3,100 members residing off reserve. The community of Wabasca is home for 2,500 band members and approximately 2,500 Métis and non-Aboriginal community members.

Bigstone's level of education is typical of the challenge facing Aboriginal communities. For the population aged fifteen years and older, INAC statistics indicate, 39 per cent have less than grade nine; 36 per cent have grade nine to thirteen (90 per cent did not graduate from grade twelve); 3 per cent hold trades certificates; 15 per cent have non-university education, and 7 per cent are seeking university degrees. Training is crucial if community members are going to participate in development projects. According to Rick Allen, director of Economic Development for the band, in 1997 the community spent between $800,000 and $1 million on training. "Our employability rate is probably 50 per cent right now, but I can see us hitting 75 per cent in five years," Rick says. "Companies have to cooperate with us on this and stop trying to cut us out of the picture. Training is critical for us, but it is not as cost effective to them."

The community is focusing on opportunities with oil and gas, forestry, and tourism. These activities fall under the purview of Bigstone Cree Enterprises Ltd., formed in the early 1980s as part of the move to take the Nation closer to self-government and self-reliance. Major projects have involved partnering with Amoco Canada and building an alliance with Al Pac. Commitment at all levels of company management to make such initiatives work has resulted in steady employment for fifty members, seasonal employment for up to 130 members, and business opportunities for local companies.

At this point, effectiveness is not compromised by having the chief and council members on the board of these enterprises. Chief Mel Beaver notes that many decisions involve using political leverage. It is an asset to be able to move quickly and make those decisions as required.

Past leadership started work on a solid foundation for current leadership to build on successfully. Chief Beaver notes that the very reason for the existence of chief and council is to improve the quality of life and health of people in the community. "The reason why we get involved in issues is to make it better for everyone, especially the youth," he says. "We want them to have many opportunities today. We are paving the way to creating jobs for them as we encourage them to get trained and more educated over the next five or ten years. We speak specifically of opportunities in oil, gas, forestry, and tourism. We consistently try to phase in young people and our recent graduates into current projects. We are examining ways to maintain good communications with them when they are away studying. We want them to know they are welcome."

JOURNEY TO SELF-SUFFICIENCY

Since the takeover of programs in 1978 from the Department of Indian Affairs, Bigstone Cree Nation has seen changes. Chief and council now total seven, down from thirteen. While some people in the community questioned the wisdom of taking over programs, many had positive attitudes. Chief Beaver recalls:

Most of the council thought who better to know what is best than us? The worst that can happen is that we make some mistakes. The government has made worse mistakes than we have. We hire our own people, train our own people, and work to getting them to where they can head programs as directors or managers.

Employment issues were important. We wanted to control our economy where we are able to plan and make local decisions. We wanted to reduce administrative costs and use those dollars elsewhere. It was exciting, but we had to deal with dissent in the community. Today we are experiencing another large growth period. I am confident we have the skills to guide an expansion in services. We have many years of experience, so there is no way to go but forward in terms of our growth at Bigstone.

Effective self-government generally includes encouraging community input. Regular community meetings provide such opportunities in Bigstone Cree Nation. Traditionally, the advice of elders is sought in matters important to community welfare – in particular, in education and social affairs. They are an important group of advisors. Chief Beaver sums up recent discussion on accountability and responsibility: "Council said in the end that chief and council are held accountable and responsible for all decisions that are made. We may make them, or our elders when we delegate that right to them, but when the dust settles, it is the chief and council that are responsible and accountable to the community. If we were ever in a situation of conflict with the elders and their advice, we would not disregard their input, but chief and council would have to agree on the best decision. "

In achieving goals for the community, economic development initiatives are very important. Some issues to be considered in their development strategies include an outstanding land claim, community attitudes, environmental protection, training programs, and the contributions of women.

Unsettled land claims lend uncertainty to the business environment and are not conducive to new development. Bigstone Cree Nation invites companies wanting to do business on their traditional land to join them in working out a settlement to their land claim. They argue that it is in everyone's best interests to support a quick resolution and that companies should build in costs of settlement into projects, since it is an investment that will be worthwhile. Future costs from an unsettled claim are high because they include human costs.

Rick Allen advises senior management in any corporation they deal with that "they are operating in areas that may very well be land claim areas and that the people here have the right to work and train. We suggest that they are better off working with our people since it saves money on extra expenses. We also let them know that down the road, when the land claims are settled, we may come back on them through legal means if we are ignored."

Rick is convinced that Bigstone Cree Nation must constantly protect its interests in the face of corporate disinterest.

"What I see happening is that corporate presidents and vice presidents embrace mandates to support First Nations, but that does not always trickle down to the supervisors or consultants," he says. "All they care about is the bottom line, so they will get us to sign on the dotted line and then turn around and give us reasons why they can't use us, like, it is too expensive. Once that happens, we try to resolve it locally, but if it that doesn't work then we go directly to senior management."

Industry has historically been viewed with distrust in Bigstone. Chief Beaver recalls the concerns expressed at Al Pac environmental impact assessment hearings held in 1988 through 1990:

They asked communities about a response to plans to clear-cut this part of northern Alberta. Our chief and council were against Al Pac's plans because of the devastation clear-cut logging has on the land. We organized a panel discussion to give the other side. We had a B.C. chief come and tell about his community's experience with clear-cut logging. He talked about the promise of job training, but when the dust settled, the company didn't hire locally since people didn't have the skills. He painted a bleak and negative picture of forestry companies.

Today is different. The leadership gives priority to development and to the environment. We give the community our perspectives on how we see those two priorities coexisting. The community understands our long-term plans for development. We want to establish a working relationship with companies while paying attention to membership concerns about land use. For these reasons, I think that people are more receptive to development than before. This includes development opportunities with forestry companies like Al Pac.

Bigstone Cree Nation works to establish successful training opportunities with industries operating locally. The oil industry has been active. Amoco, for example, gave enough contracts to Bigstone Cree Enterprises that Enterprises were able to reduce their rates to be more competitive and cover the costs of training community members. Chief Beaver is pleased with how things have worked out. "We have a relationship with Amoco that sees them send any outside company working for them to the band. The band puts them to work under Bigstone Cree Nation Enterprises. We get a percentage, and that money is used for training."

Where other communities might issue dividends to community members, profits from Enterprise operations go into training. As Rick points out, "Training is not cash dividends, but it is dividends that will train our children. We tell our community that today we will train you, tomorrow we will train your children, and then we will put a portion of the money away. We invest some so that there is money there to train your grandchildren. We don't look at this as a five year program. This is a fifty to one-hundred year program."

In addition to industry partners, partnership is being cultivated with the surrounding non-Nation member community. According to Chief Beaver, the history of cooperation between the on-reserve and off-reserve communities is poor. There have been some successful efforts however, on a small scale. "We met recently about starting more small projects in order to establish our relationship and then go from there," he says. "The response from off-reserve leadership is quite positive. With the oil and gas development or even forestry occurring now, we could work and stand together as a community. We could be more effective as a bunch of local contractors going to these companies together." These partnerships can be extended to local business. In this way, expertise can be shared, competition will be minimized, and training opportunities can be optimized.

At the macro-economic level, the global economy impacts on Bigstone Cree Nation through industry. For example, Al Pac is owned by a Japanese company, although Rick notes that he has never seen a Japanese person from the parent company in their community. In his opinion, there is an indifference to Aboriginal concerns at the global level that is important to recognize. "The Japanese don't care about Indian rights issues," he says. "It is not a knock on Japanese in general, nor are they necessarily racist. It is just simply that they don't care. They do business around the world. We know the Alberta government has invested hundreds of millions of dollars in Al Pac – all the more reason that they should have to work with us, since the Japanese are basically working with taxpayer dollars."

The leadership must balance environmental protection concerns of the community with the need for jobs, and weigh the push to develop resources by industry against all the attendant negative environmental impacts. It is a quandary without easy answers. Chief Beaver comments on the Bigstone strategy and the background leading to its development:

In the early 1990s, our community placed emphasis on development because development was finally here in our region. We wanted to be a part of it and take advantage of it through Bigstone Enterprises. On one hand we enjoy the development that is happening and the benefits, but at the same time the downside is troubling in terms of the effects on our water, air, land, trees, and so on.

Bigstone council talks about these issues on a regular basis. We recently completed a land-use study in order to deal with our land-claim and development issues. A group of researchers worked with our people and identified how our people used the land. They located berrying sites, our old graveyards, and where we used to hunt, fish, and trap. When we looked at the map with all the things that our people used to do in our vast territorial land, it underlined the need for us to pay closer attention to protecting the land and making the environment a priority when we talk to companies about development.

When we meet with the resource companies that work in our area, we say that development is fine, but the environment is also a priority. We expect them to pay attention to our land-use study. We don't want to chase them away, but we also love our environment. We ask companies to be our partners not only in development but also in making sure that we don't destroy the environment.

This is the type of up-front dialogue we have with the companies on a regular basis. Their response is mainly positive, and they want to work with us. We know they want to make their money, but in order to do that, they need a positive and a productive working relationship with the leadership and the community people here. We are pretty straightforward with them.

In taking an holistic view to development and environment, Bigstone understands that this attitude means encouraging each community member to join in wholeheartedly in making a difference. The contribution of Bigstone's women to making the community healthy and productive is significant. Their participation permeates all aspects of community life.

Chief Mel Beaver has taken an interest in this area:

A lot of what I believe or say is a result of my upbringing. I see women as being an important part of me, including my mother and my grandmother. As a result of how I was raised, I see women as being a very important contributing factor to the community here. On the political scene we have had women on council in the past. They are in the office and also in the community.

I look at the strength of some of our female elders, for when they talk, our people listen. They are our hidden leaders who have influence in the home and in community meetings. They don't hold titles or positions, but they are leaders at different levels at home and in the community. The way that I see it, the women have a very active and substantial role in our community. Even though we have some real macho men who don't believe that women should hold powerful positions, I think they are starting to think otherwise.

In summary, Bigstone Cree Nation is working hard to develop the community in terms of encouraging all members to be part of their goal of self-sufficiency. They are dealing with obstacles openly and up front, in the community and with industry representatives. They try to walk a fine line of doing business while protecting the environment as directed by the community. They focus on cooperation and partnership.

"I think that people are expecting development to continue in a controlled way that is based on what they think is important," says Chief Beaver. "They value the environment, for example, and they don't want us to sell out to development. As long as the leadership pay attention to our people's values and beliefs, then I see good things happening here. I think the way that this community is evolving is very positive."

ALBERTA PACIFIC FOREST INDUSTRY INC.

In this section, Al Pac is examined as an example of a company doing business on the traditional lands of the Bigstone Cree. Formed in 1988, Al Pac operates in northeastern Alberta as a wholly owned subsidiary of Crestbrook Forest Industries. As part of the process of getting its licence, Al Pac participated in a series of environmental impact assessment hearings in the communities in their forestry management area (FMA). One very strong message was that Al Pac must be prepared to work with the Aboriginal communities. The senior managers at that time were amenable to creating a company that would be unique in the industry. They set about gathering a team of individuals who had expertise in their respective fields and who could work with a mandate that included building strong relationships with the Aboriginal communities in their FMA. This goal was incorporated into their mandate, addressing a distinct business ethic and relationships with all communities in the FMA.

The new mill was operational in 1991–92. Bill Hunter, acting general manager in 1997, recalls the start-up: "Jerry Fenner, senior vice-president at the time, and several other vice-presidents had a vision to take all of the historical garbage of what our industry has created to see if we can follow the best available method of management. We decided to participate with the communities. The owners said, 'Go for it, since we need a well-run mill. We absolutely need to operate at peak performance, production quality, and environmental safety. The trade-off is that we will stand back and support you financially.'"

The forestry industry is not generally interested in taking a proactive stance in developing relationships with communities. Ken Plourde, a forest resources business leader, has worked in the industry in British Columbia for a number of years. Al Pac is "ten miles ahead of the rest," in his opinion. "We are a brand new company, and we have, a new focus. In my experience, the general attitude of a forestry company coming into a new area is that we've got the right to be here and you will automatically like us because we provide jobs. Companies are probably astounded when somebody doesn't like what they are doing. They don't want to believe it. They haven't really been sensitive to the human aspect in the past. I think companies are treating people better, as a spin-off of society becoming more tolerant."

In Ken's experience, there is little left for communities once a company comes, extracts its products, and then leaves. When companies plan to work in an area for an extended period of time, however, there are more opportunities to mitigate the impact of their activities on the environment and the people.

Al Pac is interested in making sure that other forestry companies in Alberta have assistance in working with local communities. They have been monitoring the controversial situation between the Lubicon Cree Nation and Daishowa, a Japanese-owned forestry company. Daishowa's focus is on technology and the plant, with little attention on communities. "We don't want to be painted with the same brush," says Bill Hunter. "We want industry in Alberta, and more especially the forestry industry, to be accepted and respected in the same way. It should not matter which company you are from. We share a lot of ideas and we meet in order to build strategies."

According to Bill, in order to successfully develop a community focus, someone within the company must a champion it. "A champion has to have passion, empathy, and a heartfelt need to develop new relationships. Since everything is bottom-line oriented in business, a champion will ensure these programs survive in tight economic times. It is a constant battle to protect some of our existing programs because as you have heard in the media, we have missed a few loan payments. Capital is tight, and we need to make very drastic cuts to survive these very, very tough times." At Al Pac, several senior managers were the champions for working with Aboriginal communities. Supporters throughout operations have worked to implement policies in areas including employment, community liaison, and supplier standards that lead to strong, healthy relationships.

In Ken's view, these policies make good business sense:

For one thing, it makes good business sense that when you go into somebody else's area and start doing something, the most humanitarian thing you can do is talk to the people there, discuss the negative and positive impacts that you bring their way.

Secondly, it makes sense to identify people who share the same vision. This includes educating community people about the vision and then giving them the opportunity to participate as employees or suppliers. You require the right kind of people to bring groups together internally and externally.

Finally, for companies not interested in the human aspect, securing their raw material supply is critical to continued operations. For example, if there is political unrest in the communities and their supplies are affected, then their operations may be shut down.

Establishing a working relationship with communities is an ongoing process that takes time and planning. At the beginning this wasn't easy, Bill says, as Al Pac was new to the neighborhood. "We had to win their respect and build relationships in these communities. The oil and gas industry has been here for a very long time. We are the first major forestry corporation here in the northeast section of the FMA. We wanted to do it right, so we brought together a group of people who have the expertise but more specifically have the drive to make a difference. We created the Aboriginal Affairs Resource Team (AART). Today we are very happy with the progress, but we still have a long way to go."

To head AART, Al Pac hired an Aboriginal consultant, Elmer Ghostkeeper. Elmer is from northern Alberta, knows the land, and has his culture and language. He introduced Al Pac's management team members to chiefs and councils and community people throughout the FMA. Bob Rualt, general manager of operations, recalls the process:

We wanted to understand what they were doing and get them to try to learn what we were about. We had to build trust too. We demonstrated trust by listening to them, going out there and being very open to their questions. We tried to answer them, and if we didn't know the answers, then we said so. We didn't beat around the bush.

Initially, Bigstone was very pro-environment and wasn't interested in the mill. Other communities like Janvier were open-minded and wanted to work with us. We had to learn about what was important to the communities. We implemented cultural studies for our employees. We talked with community members in order to understand their traditional values regarding the land. We learned about the place that trapping holds in their economy and the major challenge to keep it going. We learned about their values, politics, and social structures.

Their number-one economic challenge is never-ending. Jobs, jobs, jobs is the number-one challenge. They aren't educated, but they do have the desire to do work. We need time for job training, building partnerships, and offering contracts of all kinds.

AART's main function is to act as a resource and provide a liaison between corporate teams and communities. AART also manages a trappers' compensation program and has facilitated a variety of projects including a loan circle and a land-use study. Another company initiative of interest is a memorandum of understanding (MOU) with Bigstone Cree Nation.

Mandatory cultural education programs help Al Pac employees understand issues currently faced by Aboriginal communities. They also learn about community priorities. Aboriginal perspectives are compared to the western science worldview. Employees have the opportunity to participate in a sweat-lodge ceremony offered by an elder who is an AART member. For many Al Pac employees this ceremony has become very meaningful and special in their work. If there is any resistance to the policy, it is not visible, and senior management is pleased with how well people are honouring the policy.

AART is a relatively unique initiative in the forestry industry although community leaders are now requesting that other companies operating in their area have an Aboriginal Affairs group. It is important that AART members have knowledge of communities and have expertise; for example, they are from the area and may be former chiefs or trappers and hunters. They are sensitive to community needs while operating within the corporate context. Misunderstandings can be handled with sensitivity or avoided altogether. For this to happen, key policy aspects must be in place, Bob notes:

The number-one challenge, generally, is to have commitment to your policy regarding Aboriginal people in your corporation from the bottom to the top. You have to have the attitude that everyone has equal opportunity to your job. It is a challenge.

AART has some autonomy in decision making, team building, and bringing their culture to the team. They are accountable to their team, and they need a reasonable budget to support their activities. In our case there is a million-dollar budget for them. AART is part of the company business plan. They have to be accepted by the other teams.

They have opened the door to the communities, and the company has to be prepared to go there and participate. Sometimes it is tough, but you have to do that.

Bill adds:

We have got good rapport with most of the communities. On a couple of occasions some of them were hostile but with good reason. We go into the communities and talk to the elders, community and political leaders, and other leaders. Through these relationships we explore opportunities or engage in contracts. Initially we did a mental checklist when we met, but now it is more comfortable. Our team know who to contact when they go into an area, and they do it automatically as part of operations. When there is a change in leadership, we call on the new leaders.

We have our ups and downs. We have some individuals who are not really pleased with the progress that we are making. They think it is too slow and that we are really not doing anything for anybody. They are probably right, so you have to listen to these people even though they are detractors.

We are careful, because some seldom offer alternative solutions. Usually they are a very small minority. Some are self-serving, and [these] can be found in Aboriginal and non-Aboriginal communities. They go away if you come up with something for them personally, and they really don't care about the rest.

As part of its trappers' compensation program, AART has specialists who talk to the trappers in the area. They administer a program that compensates for disruption of the traplines due to forestry operations. Unfortunately there is no compensation for loss of habitat, but there are information sessions and one-on-one meetings to discuss concerns.

Walter Quinn is a trapper specialist with AART. "For many, many years," he says, "the trapper has been left behind, but with Al Pac our number-one priority is to help the 426 trappers in the FMA in any way we can. Our work does devastate traplines, and we would have to deal with trappers one way or another. While you can't make a living at trapping, it is a good hobby or for recreational purposes. I used to trap, and many times companies will just push your traps away to the side.

They don't honour the special places. Your family may have lived in an old cabin for many years. You don't want that pushed away, because the memories are special. We try to avoid those kinds of incidents. We deal directly with the trappers to avoid any problems."

Another program to support community economic development involved a loan circle to support a small sawmill. The idea was to provide financial assistance to local business development. A substantial sum was invested in the sawmill, but for a number of reasons the program was put on hold. Al Pac has intentions to revive the program when circumstances are deemed appropriate so that they can make a positive contribution to economic development projects.

Al Pac also supported a project that focused on traditional land use in the FMA by Bigstone Cree Nation. The sacred areas that were identified included traditional hunting and gathering areas, burial sites, and ceremonial locations. Al Pac uses this information in the planning process and Bigstone Cree Nation uses it in planning resource development on their traditional lands. The project begins to show the level of human activity in a way that many people can understand.

This traditional land use study is only one source for the long-term plan that Al Pac works up with the assistance and input of a task force. That task force involves community people from all walks of life including community people, trappers, hunters, fishers, elders, and, originally, environmentalists. This plan is important and is reviewed in community meetings, in which the annual plan and the plans for the next twenty years are proposed so that people have a chance to share their reactions.

Another significant move between Bigstone and Al Pac is a memorandum of understanding (MOU) to recognize on paper the relationship they would like to cultivate. Al Pac chose Bigstone for the MOU because of the working relationship and Bigstone's size: they are a large enough community for such a partnership to be workable. The MOU is simple and sets out a partnership based on mutual intentions. It can only work, however, if both parties are clear about expectations and want to work together. Al Pac has not entered into any other MOUs because of the resource investment that is required and the fact that other communities don't have sufficient numbers or the level of workforce that Bigstone demonstrates.

After several years, both partners give a mixed review of the MOU and are focusing on how to improve the partnership. Rick Allen, Bigstone's economic development manager, thinks the MOU is a good thing, but, he says, "You really have to make sure that you have got the fine points nailed down. The MOU obligates companies to work with Bigstone Enterprises, but they have to back it up. I think the MOU with Al Pac has been very poorly supported. When we entered the MOU, Al Pac was supposed to operate a certain amount of production, which would then create a certain amount of work for us." Within a few weeks in the first year, however, Rick was told that Al Pac had worked out a new technology and didn't need as much lumber as they thought for production at the mill. "Is it true?" Rick wonders. "I don't know. All I know is that when the MOU was signed, we expected to get a certain amount of work. We didn't want to hear a story that they do not require that much work. That is not satisfactory."

In Ken Plourde's opinion the partnership agreement is only good if both parties want it to work and understand what they are getting into:

The partnership is not worth two cents if there is no good will. Unfortunately, the federal government has muddied the water. Other Aboriginal people have told me this, so I can repeat it. There is a generation of spoiled people. I don't mean it to be a general statement, and it may or may not be a fair statement.

They may have thought that this MOU was going to be an easy thing. It is not, really, and it is our fault if we did not make it clear. I thought that we did. They have to produce at a certain level, maintain their machinery, and follow the other points in the MOU. They will have to work at it to succeed because this is not going to be subsidized. Training may be subsidized in the initial period but not afterwards.

Becoming self-sufficient is the goal – otherwise we have not accomplished much. Make-work projects are short term and are not the answer. Real business opportunities and focused training are the answer. It is our fault if people become disenchanted or think that it will be easy. Everyone progresses at their own speed, and they have to be ready for a partnership. We are proceeding slowly with the next MOU with lots of up-front discussion.

Sharing expectations surrounding an MOU is a starting point for discussion. Likely topics include effective leadership, partnering, selling a training component, and educating communities about Aboriginal policies. Clear understanding of what an MOU brings helps minimize misunderstanding.

SHARING PERSPECTIVES

In committing to successful long-term partnerships, it is important that both sides be open to understanding realities, pressures, and shifting priorities affecting each partner. For Bigstone, for example, other industries are operating on their traditional lands with different pay structures and business opportunities; some are more attractive than Al Pac in terms of revenue-generating opportunities. However, the partnership with Al Pac has given Bigstone good experience. Future partnerships will be more specific and will have revenue-sharing possibilities spelled out in the agreement. Meanwhile, Al Pac is going to be in their territory for many years to come, and so Bigstone is prepared to develop the partnership so that the community benefits.

For Al Pac, supporting community projects is worthwhile but time consuming and, in some instances, costly. Each partner must come back to the table again and again, with new players, sometimes covering the same ground but each time with an attitude of building a partnership. For AART employees, challenges include presenting information to the community in ways that capture their interest for ongoing sessions and on an understandable level. Sometimes the decision to work at Al Pac must be defended, with employees having their own individual reasons for working there – from wanting to support their families to seeing good corporate citizenship in decisions taken by the company.

The context in which economic development occurs in Aboriginal communities generally sees the leadership stretched thin. As previously mentioned, Bigstone has set up agreements with corporate partners that their sub-contractors work through Bigstone Enterprises. They build in 15 per cent to fund training. Some customers try to pay sub-contractors directly to cut out Bigstone and the surcharge. To curtail this type of activity, Bigstone must monitor these contracts regularly – a time-consuming activity.

Training is a tough sell, because it makes Bigstone less competitive than similar companies that do not have a training mandate. Most companies focus on the bottom line, but training takes time and resources. Bigstone has to be creative and persistent in order to meet community priorities. Chief Beaver observes:

When we approach companies about training, we are going against their mandate to make money as fast as possible. So we have to be forceful with them to make them understand that this is an investment for us and for them. It is cheaper for them to train our own people, for example, than to bring in a trained crew from Calgary. By accepting this training challenge, it is a short-term investment for a long-term gain.

It is an internal challenge for chief and council to generate as many business opportunities with training components, balancing profit with the need to train our people. Since we are meeting hesitation, the board of directors for Bigstone Enterprises is reassessing the mandate.

We have to handle training differently. We ask ourselves whether or not we should train on site rather than bothering companies, or try to train people at their site. We eventually want to operate as any other company that can do quality work for oil companies or forestry companies with training occurring but in a different way.

Al Pac is meeting a challenge of similar importance in implementing a policy that favours Aboriginal people for employment, from out-sourcing to creating a special department focused on their needs. Bill reflects on this challenge:

Canada is a great nation made up of a potpourri of cultures, but there is no doubt that there is still racism here. I am not talking in terms of hatred, but I am talking about recognizing differences between people. From time to time I do have team members within the manufacturing plant here at Al Pac asking "Why do we focus on Aboriginal content? When I walk into the vestibule, why is it full of Aboriginal arts and crafts, and why do I have to spend time with AART?" It is almost like favouritism. Why don't we spend the same amount of time supporting and trying to understand the white Russian colony that lives just thirty kilometres east of us, or the Lebanese, Ukranian, or any other cultural group?'

Our reply is that the predominant community in our FMA is Aboriginal, and we want to work with them successfully. There is a lot to learn about Aboriginal people. We want to understand why they think the way they do and make the types of decisions they do. Our long-term strategy is full integration at the mill. Some day there is going to be an Aboriginal person sitting in this chair, running this company. That will lead to security of this operation and security of this business because it is totally supported by the people in the FMA. Environmentalists, business, and government won't stand a chance.

It does not have to be 100 per cent run by Aboriginal people, but it has to have the commitment, the direction, and the vision that incorporate Aboriginal needs and wisdom. I implemented a program that allows Aboriginal people priority in working in eight positions through a program of reserved occupancy. Based on my background, it is clear to me that it does not matter if you are Aboriginal, Ukrainian, or Russian – if you come from a community where you grew up all your life and you have to move one hundred or two hundred kilometres to begin work in a giant industrial complex like this, there is a high fear factor.

It is an unbelievable obstacle. So to enhance opportunities for Aboriginal people, they are gradually exposed to the modern technical world in ways that make them feel more comfortable. They have a schedule with certain goals. As they start to warm up, they start to look around the mill and notice other jobs and possibilities for themselves. I think we have been quietly successful. We have had at least thirty to thirty-five people come through the system. Some are taking advantage of the opportunities and moving into higher-profile jobs with more job-skill requirements. That is exciting. They like the steady income and report that their families have finally adapted to the move. Others commute from their home communities because they like the steady income. Others say it is too stressful and don't stay on.

We set this opportunity up so that they can make decisions about working with us on their time. I don't want failure for them. I don't want failure for us. I don't want failures for me personally. I want Aboriginal employees to know for themselves that they can handle the responsibility, that they are supported in a team environment, and that they have peers from their own culture. I like it that way.

In conclusion, making a partnership work is like a marriage. The relationship takes a lot of work and the right attitudes. It takes renegotiation and realistic expectations about what is possible over what time frame. It takes policies that build on each other in both the internal and external operating environments. For Al Pac, it makes good business sense for many reasons to work with the Aboriginal communities in their FMA. In the long term, getting the community to buy into their operations will secure their future. This will have spin-off security for the communities that local Al Pac employees support.

For Bigstone Cree Nation, Al Pac is one of many companies that will help secure future self-sufficiency. Besides resource development, they are focusing on the health field, with their own pharmacy and supporting services. The leadership works hard to make development a reality but without losing sight of the priorities of their community members. Training and the environment come first in all their projects.

For Chief Beaver, his personal philosophy is to be honest, cooperative, and straightforward in all his dealings with business and his community. This sets the stage for a strong partnership and avoids problems due to lack of trust. He is proud of his community and optimistic for the future:

I am confident that the future will bring good things for this community. We've gone through some growing pains and lack of confidence in leadership over the years. I was a part of that leadership, so I blame myself. Now I have a good sense that the council members and I want to do right things for the people.

Our community has higher expectations for its leadership. They are sick and tired of people doing the wrong things. I give credit to the former chief and council for the last three to four years of tremendous growth and development. I think people are expecting that development will continue in a controlled way that is acceptable to them based on what they think is important. Their regard for the environment is paramount, and we are not going to sell out to development.

So long as the leadership pay attention to people's values, beliefs, and priorities, I think that this community will evolve a strong partnership of economic development with industry.

9

St Theresa Point, Manitoba, and The North West Company

In the early 1990s, ST THERESA POINT entered into an agreement with The North West Company. The community is a large one with an employment rate of 10 to 15 per cent. More than half the population is young people. Chief Reggie Mason says that the community's goal is to take care of themselves, using their own resources so they no longer need the government. In keeping with that goal, ownership of local business is important. This includes the opportunity to own a mall that was financed by TNWC and where the company pays lease payments.

The North West Company acquired the northern-based stores from the Hudson's Bay Company. Their focus is on the North, and they are proud of their Aboriginal employment record. They are creative in fostering customer loyalty and dedication, both in their employees and their market. Aboriginal shareholders are sought aggressively. Creative ways of supporting community efforts are carried out within the boundaries of proper business practice. Some insiders predict that the organization will eventually be truly an Aboriginal organization right through to senior management.

The partnership between St Theresa Point (STP) and The North West Company is complex. On one level it meets the terms of the agreements. On another level, the community feels that it is not fair and should be renegotiated. This is in keeping with a sentiment that major corporations have come into the community and generated revenue with little benefit to the community.

UNDERSTANDING THE COMMUNITY:
HEART TO HEART

Located in the north-eastern part of the province of Manitoba, St Theresa Point is a community of 2,700 people. It is accessible by air year round and by ice road for two months in the winter. Approximately 60 per cent of the community are under eighteen, and there is a 10 to 15 per cent employment rate. People live out their whole lives in STP. Their children may go out of the community to complete their schooling, but then, more often then not, they return.

According to Chief Mason, the community places emphasis on the importance of family. Everyone is made to feel welcome and a part of the community, including those who are new. There are gatherings for community feasts, traditional games, and more modern pursuits such as hockey. The extended family is important, and family elders step in to help maintain healthy families. Almost every family has a trapline and maintains a relationship with the land.

Chief Mason has been chief for two terms. He recalls with pride the history of his homeland and connection to the Creator:

The Creator put us on that land, on earth. He gave us everything to provide for ourselves. In the beginning our ancestors had everything provided for them from the land. Roman Catholic missionaries came and started a sawmill, and began building modern housing although people were still surviving off the land by fishing, trapping, hunting moose, and tending small potato and vegetable gardens. The Hudson's Bay Company was the only company in the area and traded for furs at Island Lake [a nearby community].

Eventually social assistance was introduced and the many concerns of a growing population. Today our schools are overcrowded, and roads are dusty and unhealthy for our kids in the summertime. The cost of living is very high because we are isolated. Most residents are on social assistance and live in deteriorating housing. We don't have the housing supplies needed to renovate and improve conditions. The lack of jobs causes social problems, and the youth get into trouble.

We must follow our own principles of survival, which means we must use our resources as much as we can to provide for ourselves including housing, clothing, and food and to build our economy.

The first priority for the community is to pursue self-governance; they wish to reclaim responsibility for their traditional lands. Part of the process was begun with the 1994 treaty land entitlement agreement, which has meant some of their land will be returned. The land is currently under provincial jurisdiction and will be turned over to the federal government to designate as reserve land. This is not all of the community's traditional territory, so they hope to make a comprehensive land claim, although that process is severely backlogged.

With the land will come the means to support themselves. Chief Mason describes his introduction to the idea of land ownership, traditionally a foreign concept, and talks about the impact of taking responsibility for the land again for STP:

I was a young kid with some friends. We went fishing, and we stopped to build a fire on an island in Island Lake which we thought was everyone's, so we could cook our lunch. The province had leased the land to a man. We thought the land was ours, and that man started throwing rocks and shouting, "Get off my land!" That triggered me to think about what I want for our people.

Economic development is important to our community. We need to finalize our land claims so that we can utilize our resources for ourselves with the help of companies or industry. We would invite a lumber company and we would harvest our resources together. It would provide employment for our community.

A lot of people in our community feel that they want to be productive and contribute, but they have no choice but to be on welfare. They want to have an economic base like fishing, for example. Due to our isolation, our fish are not marketable as a sustainable resource. We have to freight it out, and it is expensive. We wouldn't make a profit. So instead, we need an all-weather road to access an economic base in our area. There are also minerals inside our reserve boundaries.

We will maintain our connection to the land with this development that will allow us to be life-sustaining. We have our own ways of looking at our environment. Our elders are gifted in that area. They know the river and the currents in the lake and how we can use the water for transport. They know what can be destroyed and what must be protected. There is a lot of concern for our land and our resources.

Regaining control of the land and having access to the resources will go a long way towards regaining better community health. In the meantime, the community supports programs and volunteers to address some of the problems. The church is very active in these efforts and has the support of the young people. Chief Mason views it as a sign of a spiritually healthy community that STP members are respectful of the church and of traditional prayer. Mike Flett, a community member and director of Childcare, says that the elders were taught by the sisters of the church, and most of them maintain close ties with both tradition and the church. "We do not want to lose our traditional ways in the future, for that is what keeps us strong," Mike says. "Without our traditional food and medicines we would become weak. We need to live by the land, for with respect for the land comes respect for life. If someone from outside wants to understand this, then they too must live by the land."

In addition to building the all-weather road and developing the lumber and fishing industries, STP would like to build a sawmill and a fish plant. They want to own a bush plane service, a heavy trucking company and their own small airline. Chief Mason says that community members are already training for positions in these projects. They would like to attract industry partners since they have few assets to contribute. Chief Mason states emphatically, "This is our home and we're not leaving. We have to protect our land through our spiritual, traditional, and customary laws. The spirit of our ancestors is with us. Sometimes it is hard to continue, but we must maintain this area."

Training and education are critical to the future of the community. Mike regularly visits classrooms to share community plans and encourage young people to complete their education. There are 850 children in school from kindergarten to grade ten. Problems with fungus contamination have closed the school, and children have lost many days. Teachers and children are both frustrated. It is hard to maintain progress in education when faced with such obstacles. The government has done little to rectify the situation.

School is important, but meanwhile the loss of culture and traditions is a hard fact of modern life. This situation is being improved as people from the community are trained as educators and return to STP to teach. David McDougall, vice-principal of the school and a community member, recalls the important lessons he learned from his family:

I think that we have lost a good portion of our culture because of such things as welfare. The lessons I learned growing up helped me. At nine or ten I was on the dog-sled gathering wood. At about fourteen years of age my father used to take me to the bush for two months at a time out of the school year. I had to do my school work, as that was the number-one thing for my father. He believed that whatever you are doing, don't take on so much that you can't handle it. If you can handle it, then do it, because you will realize your full potential.

When I went down south for high school, it was my Dad's energy as well as his enthusiasm for success, regardless of what I was doing, that helped me through the tough times. I am very lucky since the work ethic was stressed at home – none of this "that is the white man's way." It does not matter where you are, you could be in the midst of white faces, you will never change who you are. But you can function anywhere, given the right tools and the right attitude. You can make a contribution to people. It does not matter what colour their faces are, because you still are doing good.

My grandfather used to tell me that I couldn't live my life the way that he lived his life, but I could live by the same principles. He said that I couldn't live the same life that my white mentor had, but I can have the best of both worlds. I can chart my own course, and as long as I do things well, there is no way that I can get off course. I can make a lot of mistakes along the way because that is how we learn, but in the end I will do more good if I do my best.

Educational success requires commitment on the part of both parents and students. This is something that many families still have to work at, so that their children are ready to take advantage of the opportunities to work in the community. Education has been a mixed blessing for David, whose experience is not that different from many who have returned to their communities. Their challenge has been to come to terms with those people whose education stopped early and who are offended by those they label as educated "know-it-alls." This makes it difficult to contribute to the community at times, but it has to be handled in diplomatic ways.

Education of community youth is critical for STP's future. The close-knit, family-focused community is concentrating on many issues that will affect its goals for economic development.

DEVELOPING RESOURCES
AND GROWING SMALL BUSINESS

Chief Mason knows that the people of STP want to address their own needs rather than have government be in charge of housing, roads, and infrastructure needs. Economic development would give the community the means to take control. At present there is hesitation over developing resources, David says, because of the respect for the land, the people, and the culture. He thinks the community will be able to balance the need for reasonable development without sacrificing cultural and traditional practices of First Nations people.

The band owns a number of businesses, and several small privately owned businesses are in operation. The North West Company owns a Northern store, located in a mall in the community, that provides employment for a number of local people. Band-owned businesses include a restaurant and convenience store in the mall, a bulk fuel supplier, a residence for visitors, and STP Broadcasting, which provides radio programming. The band also owns a project management company and leases an airplane for STP Airlines. Clarence Mason, a community member and the director of Economic Development, notes that these companies are in better economic shape after a department review of management practices. Access to management skills is poor and creates problems for these businesses, Clarence says. "We are lacking a pool of managers that are qualified to run those businesses. We are working on that by trying to get Red River Community College business administration courses to start in the community. We will have a pool of managers for when we need them. We will have more people staying in training programs in the community than if they have to leave for training. They get homesick and leave the training before they are finished."

The convenience store struggles to compete with the Northern store by not duplicating items. Clarence estimates that almost two dozen people have tried small businesses in the past. Local women have tried catering and handicrafts. Small businesses were started in the mall but did not receive support of the community because they could not match prices of goods in the Northern store. Several gas bar owners offer fuel at the same prices but compete on the basis of hours of operation; one is a family-owned operation that has a good share of the market. But the community cannot support the current number of gas bars for very long. It is hard to be competitive within the boundaries of a community that has a 10:30 P.M. curfew.

With training and financial resources, STP plans to develop tourism opportunities and operate a hotel. European and Japanese tourists enjoy wilderness experiences, and STP has the natural setting to be a draw to this market.

STP is also interested in developing partnerships. They currently partner with Northland Fuels for the bulk fuel distributorship, and they lease the Northern store building to TNWC. The costs of building the store and the mall were financed by TNWC in a fifteen-year agreement for paying off the store so that it eventually becomes a community asset. In addition to its lease payments, TNWC offers a management training program to the community. Its only non-Aboriginal employee is the store manager, and the quality of the staffing suggests that an Aboriginal store manager is possible within the next five years.

THE NORTH WEST COMPANY PARTNERING WITH
ABORIGINAL PEOPLES

The North West Company was formed in 1987 and purchased the Hudson's Bay Company's northern operations, carrying on HBC's long history of trading in Canada. TNWC now has 150 stores operating in remote communities with a majority of Aboriginal residents across the territories and the provincial mid-North, and another twenty-five in Alaska. The company has developed a comprehensive policy that allows them to cultivate customer loyalty and build a foundation as a significant Canadian employer of Aboriginal staff.

TNWC staff interviewed for this project reflected sensitivity to broad Aboriginal issues balanced with business realities. As Paul Hughes, director of employee relations, points out, "We are aware of the local politics. However, under no circumstances do we ever become involved. At the end of the day, our role as guests in the community is to provide a service that is focused on selling food and general merchandise."

How does TNWC define its responsibilities in doing business with Aboriginal peoples, in light of the demands placed on it by Aboriginal leadership? Many of the staff are of Aboriginal heritage and have experienced growing up in small communities with Aboriginal peoples or have family in those communities. Their connections with Aboriginal issues have been formalized within TNWC and integrated into operations throughout the company. An advisory group made up of experienced senior Aboriginal political and business-people provides guidance to TNWC's senior management.

The company approaches new communities cautiously. Often the original store is located on land outside the community that in some cases is owned by the First Nations. If not, TNWC may sell the land to the community for a dollar so long as they can rent the store and supply the community. Alternatively, they may try to negotiate building a new store closer to their customers. Once they have been invited into the community, they are interested in encouraging local employment and promoting customer loyalty. Edward Kennedy, the company's president and chief executive officer, reflects on the legacy of HBC, with its positive and negative aspects: "There is a legacy, but if we don't play with the truth and [we] acknowledge the part of the legacy that we think is legitimate, then we can try to harness the experience as an example of innovation and enterprise – in other words, the northern part of the HBC history that we try to use today in a very positive way. We think there was a partnership, and it also feeds into our current thinking of the community development role that we play."

TNWC has had significant success with hiring locally. It has become the norm to fill positions from within their market area rather than automatically bringing someone in from southern Canada. Says Edward, "I am proud of the fact that we have 144 Aboriginal management people out of 650 – or an overall Aboriginal management employment rate of 24 per cent – who are moving up through supervisory department managers and store managers positions. (That figure excludes our head office staff). It sends a signal that we support the community in more ways than just providing products and services. It says that the quality of the employment is starting to reflect the people that we serve." Vice-president Len Flett's response to criticism of TNWC is to note that the North is their business and that is where they invest their time and energy.

Local people tend to want to stay in the North so there is lower turnover than with those who are hired from the South. Sometimes it is tough to fill opportunities in head office in Winnipeg because northerners do not want to move south.

Len has worked his way up through the company over a thirty-year period. He recalls that when he was manager of Native employment, anything with the word "Native" or "Aboriginal" in it was forwarded to his desk. That has changed significantly with the integration throughout the company of responsibility for working with Aboriginal people. Len is a role model for other Aboriginal employees and an example of what is possible with effort and hard work. This is important because Aboriginal people with strong educational backgrounds now have many opportunities including their band office, large companies, and government. The retail sector is notoriously low paying, so the career opportunities there have to be obvious.

Len's position when recruiting is based on his understanding of community needs. "It is the lack of management training that is holding up our movement for self-sufficiency and economic development at the grass-roots level," he says. "So, realizing that there is a lack of management skills within the Aboriginal community as a whole, I have always presented these employment opportunities as an opportunity to develop managerial skills that are also transferable. We have hired and trained a lot of good people who are going on to run and operate band programs." Some companies might be concerned about the turnover in that scenario, but there are long-term benefits to the company to have skilled, knowledgeable people in the community who are familiar with the way the company works.

Len says he has remained with TNWC because they gave him an opportunity to show what he could do. He is very competitive and has enjoyed the challenge. There are no double standards for employees; the same performance is expected, regardless of an individual's heritage.

While it is a challenge to encourage Aboriginal staff to leave their communities and move to head office, Mike Nolan made the move and has been with TNWC for more than ten years. He came into the company with business and marketing experience, having worked in the restaurant business for four years. He has completed his business administration diploma from college part time, and his goal is to earn his MBA. Mike has worked hard in a variety of marketing positions and is currently a manager buyer in footware and outerware. He admits he found it tough at first. "I had a boss that helped. I turned to him many times when I was ready to quit. When I grow up, I want to be like Ray Falkenburg. He could walk in my office today and say 'I am quitting and I am going to work over at this other company.' I would go get a cardboard box right now, pack up my stuff, and go with that man. People say I am being groomed for bigger things. Experience in different parts of the company will make me well-rounded for the future."

An intense relationship with TNWC exists in St Theresa Point, since the company is the major business in the community. A number of local residents have been employed there for many years. George McDougall, the grocery manager, has worked with the company for fifteen years. He does not know what the next five years will bring, but he plans to stay on until he retires. When he gets the opportunity, he passes on his experience to the community's young people. He recommends that they commit to doing a good job since no one is going to hand them anything. "Enjoy the job and go for it," he says.

Bridget Flett, the retail floor manager, started with TNWC in 1982. "While there is a lot of hard work," she says, "you have to be very reliable, punctual, and sincere. You have to do public relations with the community and have good relationships with fellow employees, management, and the people at head office."

Hiring locally has been an effective policy. Store managers, despite some initial misgivings by head office that they would not be sufficiently supportive, have been behind putting local people into the management program. Any feelings that Aboriginal employees might have a different work ethic or cultural practices that would negatively affect their performance have been successfully addressed in head office too. Once southern-based employees understand company policy and have some experience with Aboriginal co-workers, preconceived notions are dispelled.

In board chairman Ian Sutherland's opinion, "Many Canadians still carry a lot of prejudice and predisposed attitudes, which will change with greater understanding of Aboriginal history, and some kind of cross-cultural training. This training could be done through the companies or in the schools." In addition, he believes, TNWC must "take the effort to hire and train Aboriginal people for employment at all levels of the organizations. They need more examples to show that the prejudice that Canadians had in the past is no longer appropriate."

Saying that there are no Aboriginal applicants with sufficient training may have been true twenty years ago, but it is a patronizing perspective that is now outdated. More and more Aboriginal people have completed relevant post-secondary education or are being brought in and successfully trained on the job. Many positions require travel as well as diplomatic skills for maintaining family connections within a community while following company policy regarding such things as credit. Employees interested in a career are willing to balance these challenges with the long-term benefits.

As TNWC works to be the top retailer in the North, they have to offset criticism that sometimes they are making money at the expense of small, poor communities. In St Theresa Point, notes Chief Mason, "We feel that the Northern is making money off of Native people. I would like to see them contribute to the community. They say that they are providing services and they have basically followed the agreement. We would like to see a stronger agreement where they would provide more benefits. Our community needs a sports facility for the youth and a workshop for the elders. We also need a traditional school for the kids where they can learn our history, values, and philosophies and receive tutoring by the elders. We need funds from companies that are making a living out of us too, like TNWC lumber companies and Manitoba Hydro. They should all give back to the community."

TNWC is making efforts to support community projects within the bounds of the company donations policy. TNWC executives take an active interest in the broader Aboriginal community because it is a long-term investment the company is making. Ian recalls:

I established a relationship with Aboriginal leaders of regional groups, and we met to discuss various things such as development of stores and specific problems in communities, including customer service, quality of merchandise, prices, and some rather sensitive political issues.

The relationship with the communities is still a strength for The North West Company that is something on which we spend a lot of time and effort. Are there problems? Yes, and there have been complaints, about non-community people who we send into work in the stores to major conflicts about ownership of our stores and the community. We have actually had to leave the community because of relations. But, normally the relations are very good and demonstrate mutual respect.

TNWC is cultivating community connections by supporting local efforts of ownership. More generally, TNWC makes presentations to Aboriginal organizations with investment capital to encourage them to become shareholders in the company. More work is needed to meet company expectations, but a recent acquisition by a consortium of Aboriginal communities and organizations in Manitoba, Saskatchewan, and the Yukon is a step in the right direction. In late July 2000, Rupertsland Holdings Inc. purchased 450,000 units, making it one of the company's largest investors. In the future, as more bands want to operate their own stores, Len predicts that TNWC's role may be to provide infrastructure as an "outside partner" involved in transportation, technology, and supplies.

One promotion that demonstrates the "buy local" objective is a cartoon of a man with a Wal-Mart bag under one arm and a Costco bag under the other. As he is driving home, he sees that the local store is closed and boarded up. He asks, "What happened to them? I thought my son could get a job with them this summer." The message of course, is that local business cannot survive lack of customer support. Customers who have little cash, however, will shop where it is most cost effective. This is one of the critical challenges facing TNWC, given other large retailers, catalogue outlets, and Internet shopping services including ecommerce.

The company welcomes competition with Arctic Cooperatives Ltd., a northern-based, community-owned chain quite similar to TWNC in many ways, including in terms of Aboriginal ownership. Ian thinks that Arctic Co-op is probably good for TNWC and good for the communities in providing a competitive retail environment. However, he objects to "the Co-op" being referred to as an Aboriginal business. "We [TNWC] have a greater percentage of Aboriginal management in our company than they do," he says. "We put more money back into the community than they do. We pay taxes to Northwest Territories and other jurisdictions that go back into the community, which the Arctic Co-op does not. We buy more goods from Aboriginal industries and artisans than the Arctic Co-op does. So we think that we put more money back into the communities than they do."

Ian points out that the government put up the capital funds to build the Co-ops. "They have to pay that back. Their ownership is not unlike ours where we get monies to build our stores from our shareholders and we have to give it back to them too. So we do not see that we are much different. As we get more and more Aboriginal shareholders, we think that we are just as much an Aboriginal company as they are and more so, because I think that we are more progressive in terms of our management development practices than they are." Senior management at TNWC includes two Aboriginal board members and an Aboriginal vice-president.

It is important to understand that Aboriginal communities have had reason to look to companies as having authority and responsibilities that go beyond normal business relations. "Historically," Ian observes, "I think Aboriginal people had the view of the Hudson Bay Company as a government. It was one of the signs of authority over Aboriginal people, not unlike the church or the government. The Royal Commission on Aboriginal Peoples final report says we did not have a normal retail store customer relationship. We were regarded somewhat as an authority or as a governmental figure." Communities thus may seek support for youth, education, or family projects from companies doing business in their areas, which perhaps the government should be providing but is not, for whatever reasons. On the other hand, from the Aboriginal community perspective, taking responsibility is a corporate obligation that is long overdue.

Ian says that for TNWC, taking a position of authority in the community is no longer relevant today. "We do not try to be the government. We try to be a good corporate citizen in the community recognizing that our relationship is as a retailer dealing with customers. The customers are very important to any retail organization."

For companies wanting to work effectively with Aboriginal people, Edward suggests first of all making a concerted effort to listen to the grass-roots and to learn the nuances of the market. This takes time and effort. There are no shortcuts. The effort, however, will help companies do better in meeting the needs of their market. There are solid business reasons to understand the aspirations and needs of Aboriginal people and to integrate them into business. This cannot be an empty public relations effort, or it will fail. Listening builds understanding. Edward notes that TNWC has learned how complex the situation is when working with the Aboriginal community; it also is important to remember that a company is a guest in the community and to be guided by that realization.

Community management boards have proven effective, with the local TNWC store manager meeting regularly with community members to discuss any concerns or ideas they have to make the store more efficient. All of these efforts help to strengthen TNWC's presence in the community. They provide the opportunity to break down stereotypes of large companies, since board members have a chance to see the types of positive things that TNWC is doing. "There are myths about how bad, exploited, nasty, or self-serving or how remote and untrusting companies are, when you really have not sat down and talked to the people that are there," says Edward. Company people "are just people who are trying to serve other people or work with other people. But we get very easily into labels and paradigms. It does not help that there is not a lot of interaction between communities and companies. When good communication happens and a certain level of familiarity develops, then it is a special feeling, because you have realized that you have broken through and are beginning to develop trust."

In conclusion, Ian's vision for the future of TNWC is to "see a company with a very strong Aboriginal ownership and leadership reflecting the ownership and the communities that we operate in." Chief Mason wants to strike a better deal that will benefit his community. This is the tension that must be negotiated away by the interested parties.

St Theresa Point is a community with heart and many plans. There are many STPs across this country. There are few small businesses and it is difficult to hang in, but their leaders continue to persevere. They try to inspire their members and in the meantime build a family-oriented place where caring and sharing are the norm. This is their home, and they will spend their lives taking care of it and each other.

TNWC has many policies that support partnerships with Aboriginal peoples, including employment opportunities, training and donations programs. The company has stock promotions designed to attract Aboriginal investors and is involved with creative community partnership agreements that give ownership to communities. Community management boards ensure an ongoing connection to communities. The North is their place of business and where they expend their effort.

TNWC has entered into a partnership agreement with STP that in the eyes of STP's leadership is not yet entirely mutually beneficial. This means that STP has raised issues with TNWC that must be negotiated in order to maintain a working relationship. TNWC's considerations when moving through these negotiations must include the precedent they may set for other Aboriginal communities seeking concessions.

10

Reflections on Living Communities

For me, true insight into another person's experience begins by moving from an intellectual understanding to one that embraces heart and spirit. In taking the journey with these people and these communities, I have come to realize the limitations of my experience of that journey. I am only able to share the brief glimpses of what I know. I can share their words spoken at the time of my research. I cannot capture all of the shades of meaning nor the changes that have occurred before or since that time.

I am humbled, however, by the scope of this project and its significance within the context I have just shared. The words open windows that have not been opened in this way ever before. Though I spoke to many members in each community, I was unable to document all their insights in the case study portion of this research. It is with respect that I honour this experience and the teachings I was given.

The Elements of Development model by Salway Black (1994) forms the first framework for understanding the diverse community experiences shared here. It provides the basis for insight into some markers for successful development that incorporate Aboriginal peoples' perspectives. It is inclusive and flexible enough to go from reserve to an urban locale. The blended approaches emerging from Aboriginal worldviews and the western approach should become clearer to the reader for these selected communities in the following evaluation. They are discussed in terms of partnerships, Aboriginal wisdom, and the author's reflections.

The First Nations Development Institute (FNDI) uses this model as a starting point for discussion and regularly revises it to suit the needs of the community clients. Once a community approaches FNDI for project funding, its members meet and may discuss their community within the context of the model in order to submit a proposal based on their assessment. This process allows for dissenting opinions to be shared and balanced decisions taken. Sometimes dissent is overridden in situations where communities rely on majority guidance, while those building consensus take time to discuss so that dissenters are given the chance to be comfortable with the final decision. This means that they can live with the decision, while not necessarily agreeing with it unreservedly.

One way to use the model is to involve project and community members in plotting a point on each axis to capture their assessment of their community's strength or weakness regarding that element. They develop a visual representation of their community profile before and replot it after the project. As a planning tool, the model is unique in its ability to incorporate an Aboriginal perspective that relies on local expertise. No outside "expert" is used to undertake this analysis on behalf of the community. The community can use the tool to represent its goals and direct its current and future objectives. Figure 2 is an example of such a community profile. The ideal shape, with each of the quadrants in balance, is a circle, as illustrated by the "ideal" example. If the plotting does not yield a circle, then the community may use the model to identify areas that need attention as demonstrated in the "snapshot" example. These examples are discussed in the "Planning Tool" section.

I take this opportunity to share my insights of some of these communities for illustrative purposes and as the basis of discussion should further work using this model continue with these communities. Their economic development strategies demonstrate the breadth of approach and level of sophistication in dealing with wide-ranging problems while remaining grounded in the particular blend of tradition, knowledge, wisdom, and vision that has grown out of each community's experience. Although my personal analysis does not include the critical local perspective needed to make this evaluation complete, it is a starting point for discussion.

Each axis in the Elements of Development model addresses dynamic aspects of Aboriginal life. The naming of each axis draws on familiar details experienced by Aboriginal peoples, but in most cases it introduces concepts very foreign to mainstream economic development. For example, spirituality and kinship are not commonly discussed in a critical analysis of successful economic development. Therein lies the strength of this model, in my opinion. It is a means for Aboriginal peoples to go beyond the mainstream perspective and to contemplate their own valid reality in the understanding of community goals for successful economic development. This approach sets the stage for reciprocity, in that mainstream business can consider how capitalism might benefit from the influence of Aboriginal worldviews.

Acknowledging the role that kinship plays in the distribution of goods and services by Aboriginal peoples reveals the inherent value of everyday development practices. Kinship is not regularly identified from a western perspective as a community asset. Its inclusion leads to a better appreciation of ancient mechanisms that still have a role in Aboriginal community economic development today. The informal economy is alive and well in the communities that form part of this study. Kinship identifies the creation and circulation of assets as well as refocuses the lens of economic development from within the community.

Integral benefits and responsibilities of living in close proximity with extended family members, such as giving haircuts in exchange for work on the car or babysitting, are usually so automatic that in-depth discussion of this aspect of community life is rare. Give-aways are connected with traditional ceremonies and are present to varying degrees among the selected communities. The practice of traditional spirituality may complement or, alternatively, be circumscribed by the presence and influence of western religions, depending on the prevailing wisdom in the community. The diversity of beliefs evident in this small selection matches the diversity noted in Aboriginal nations.

Obstacles such as religion, residential school fallout, incarceration, family breakdown and dysfunction, community disinterest, or isolation all influence the effective sharing of traditional culture and values through kinship ties. In each of the selected communities, kinship ties are recognized and fostered. However, the health of some kinship ties is for many families stretched to the limit. Each community has at least one treatment facility designed to address these issues. For many families who have moved to Winnipeg, kinship ties and the sharing of traditional culture and values have broken down in the urban setting. Those who want to hold on to kinship as a meaningful part of living in the city may replace the extended family with new friends, local community members, and those with common experience.

It is not always apparent to Aboriginal community members that a broad analysis of their assets should include kinship and the informal economy. How can the narrow economic perspective of dominant society be shaken off and the blinders lifted so that Aboriginal peoples operate from their true place of strength and not from an automatic place of inferiority?

PERSONAL EFFICACY

In answering this question, a number of continua must be considered: individual initiative balanced with community/state support, work ethic and dependence, fear and self-esteem, broad and narrow future outlook, and gifting the next generation with necessary skills, including self-confidence. There are individual community members at each point on these continua. Each community has a small contingent of entrepreneurs who have a distinctive vision for their contribution to the community and the segment of it that relies on state payments to survive.

Strong, experienced leadership is helping make a difference in these areas for the selected communities, by living self-government. For example, Tsuu T'ina Nation has a comprehensive plan for employing its current membership and encouraging its young people to seek education and stay in the community. Drop-out rates are problematic, but role models and opportunities now hold out invitations to those who might choose to stay and earn their living within the community. Each of the selected communities faces the same obstacles and tries to offer similar opportunities, with varying success.

Language programs are in place to support traditions, and elders are essential to community spirit. Leadership balances political expertise with community economic development insight in setting board representation. The Gwich'in have identified local opportunities, but many in the community are still unemployed. With a finite set of opportunities, Gwich'in youth are encouraged to gain skills but understand that their future may lie outside of the community. They are developing resources at a thoughtful, careful pace. A strong call to the land and the peaceful existence it means is more evident here than in the other selected communities. Minimized in the urban setting, it grows in importance the further communities are from larger centres.

Bigstone Cree Nation is addressing the challenges of high drop-out rates and low employment opportunities by negotiating with resource companies and increasing opportunities through partnerships. Its leadership relies on expeditious decision-making when political representation is actively involved with all economic development decisions. The leadership also brings the community into the decision process. Tsuu

T'ina and the Aboriginal community of Winnipeg have few natural resources, with Tsuu T'ina creatively managing the resources and experience they do have.

Finally, Winnipeg's Aboriginal community is attempting to make a
difference for the adults who want to work and the youth who are
dropping out. This is a major challenge which the community has identified in the Aboriginal Urban Strategy and which under-financed organizations like Aboriginal Youth With Initiative and the Aboriginal
Council of Winnipeg have tried to address. It is a question of managing
individual needs with what will build community, and for three of the
selected communities the leadership have been able to exercise influence over final decisions. For the urban community, the leadership of
many organizations face resource constraints and draining discussions
regarding competing jurisdictions that hinder forward movement.

CONTROL OF ASSETS

The land-claims agreement governing the activities of the Gwich'in has
made a difference in knocking down inherent barriers to economic development. Land title and financial compensation have given the Gwich'in
nation the means to control its future. This community was most evi-
dently excited about possibilities for the future. Community control of
their investment strategy requires that the leadership recognize their
goals in its decisions and manage the trust fund for the benefit of today's
members while protecting the legacy for future generations.

The rest of these communities are bound by the Indian Act with regards to control of their assets and subject to federal and provincial
laws. Both Tsuu T'ina Nation and Bigstone Cree Nation are building
on their business experience and the hard lessons they have had to
learn. As a result they are able to focus on economic development opportunities that twenty years ago were not available to any reserve
community. They target training programs linked to economic projects
that benefit Nation members. Tsuu T'ina's approach to dividing profits
benefits the community and all their economic development endeav-
ours, in keeping with community guidance.

In contrast, urban community members have no land base but have
access to house purchases, control of savings accounts, education
upgrading, job skills and loans that are not as easily available to reserve
community members. A strong web of Aboriginal and city non-profit
organizations that meet social, health, and economic development

needs support efforts to build a strong community. Aboriginal entrepreneurs may target the Aboriginal community market, but in order to expand, they must enter into the mainstream marketplace. The Aboriginal Business Development Centre provides support for the initial entrepreneurial process.

Traditional rights to hunt and fish are protected on reserve, as is control of the small land bases. Bigstone Cree Nation and Gwich'in members trap, hunt, and fish. To a lesser extent, urban and Tsuu T'ina Nation members engage in these subsistence activities on a recreational basis and share the proceeds with their extended family.

Many financial institutions see the potential for increasing market share with Aboriginal clients in an industry that has little to no room for growth. Financial institutions are trying to capture the personal and commercial business on reserve through greater accessibility. Tsuu T'ina Nation has built a strong relationship with its financial institution based on a record of increasing assets and reliability. While it is not possible to build an urban "community" relationship with a financial institution in the same way, Aboriginal organizations based in Winnipeg do develop banking relationships. Accessibility and flexibility remain critical issues in this area.

Increasingly a skilled, educated workforce is available as a community resource, but the training process takes time. Each of these communities is facing human resource shortages and investing in long-term education. They do have control of their education (including two schools in Winnipeg) and are thus able to deal with these issues close to home, in a manner that incorporates the amount of culture and tradition that is important to the community. In any event, their pursuit of a dignified livelihood for the members of their communities underlies all the leadership strategies.

Health care is widely available in Winnipeg for Aboriginal peoples and in Calgary for Tsuu T'ina Nation members. The Gwich'in have the most limited access to quality health-care service with Bigstone Cree Nation taking some control of its health services with a full-service drugstore and dental services. These services improve the general health of the population and their strength as a community.

Many challenges must yet be addressed. While it has taken many years to create the problems facing Aboriginal people, the broader community is impatient for reaching solutions. How do these Aboriginal communities and others get significant support from the broader community with enough room for incorporating a local perspective into the solutions?

SPIRITUALITY

The presence of religion and spirituality in a community is often an indicator of healing and contemplation of one's critical place in the universe that flows from the individual, to family, and then to the community. Religion through mainstream churches co-exists with opportunities to practice traditional spirituality in these communities. Some people have forged a blending of approaches, accommodating seemingly contradictory approaches in one strong spiritual vision. Tradition has a stronger presence in communities where there is acceptance and tolerance.

The place and distinctiveness of Aboriginal peoples in society is strongly tied to language. In many of the community-run schools, children have the opportunity to learn their language and traditional teachings. The importance of language is recognized, and in Tsuu T'ina Nation and several Aboriginal Winnipeg schools, for example, funds are earmarked for developing language resources. Organizations including the Aboriginal Languages of Manitoba (formerly the Manitoba Association of Native Languages) are also very involved.

Traditional values are integral to a variety of aspects of society. Traditional roles of elders are honoured in each of these communities, and elder contributions are acknowledged. Regaining and using their own language is respected. Decision-making works to consensus in many instances. Women hold a variety of roles in community administrative structures, including in economic development, despite obstacles of sexism and beliefs that women should have no say in those forums. Many are making their own opportunities and taking advantage of them with integrity. Women are making inroads and significant contributions in each of the selected communities.

Leaders in these communities display a variety of strengths including a positive vision for their people and strategies for making them a reality, though not always without controversy and conflict. Managing such challenges effectively, especially in ways that are truly representative of community wishes, is a sign of effective leadership. It is not always possible to please everyone, but that is a reality faced by all leaders. There are many signs of communities seeking balance in all elements of economic development outlined in the model.

In its relationship to the element of spirituality on the model, kinship links with the empowerment of community members through participation, cultural integrity, and relationships with society through the media and financial institutions. Each of these communities has mechanisms for community involvement in policy and major decisions affecting them. Some encourage dissenting comments by community members, and their leaders reach consensus on a course of action while making room for dissenters to give qualified support. Tsuu T'ina's leadership note that providing a forum where a dissenting speaker is assured of being heard helps reduce the level of frustration in the community and builds solidarity.

Tsuu T'ina Nation has an extensive process of community interaction in examining projects and progress. Its due-diligence process is comprehensive and builds on its experience and best practice. Bigstone Cree Nation relies on community input to guide decision-making and the direction of future economic development. Community opinion for developing forest resources has changed over the last ten years from strongly negative to one where economic development is considered within certain boundaries that protect the community's environment. Isolated communities have limited economic development options, so that when a company wants to develop the resources in consultation, some relationship is likely to develop over time.

The Urban Aboriginal Strategy expressed the community's concerns in a process that gave them precedence for the provincial government's consideration. The question arises as to how quickly and in how intact a form will a provincial government that has changed from NDP to Conservative to Liberal champion these recommendations? For the Gwich'in, the land-claims settlement has inspired enthusiasm for positive change in the lives of its members. People have hope and a vision for the future that is becoming part of the plans for a strong community. It is an enormous task, and the leadership must coordinate plans to move forward on all fronts while maintaining momentum. Similarly complex tasks face the other selected communities.

Social respect from Canadian society is an ongoing issue for Aboriginal nations. The national media is often quick to highlight scandals and crime in the Aboriginal community while ignoring or minimizing successful business stories or academic achievements by bright Aboriginal students. How can balanced reporting be encouraged in the media when they are so focused on "extreme" human experience as "news"? There is more balance in grass-roots Aboriginal newspapers, although their relationships with leadership can be rocky, with accusations of unfair criticism and closed door politics being made back and forth. Similar issues

Figure 2. Plotting a Community's Strengths Using the Elements of Development Model for Planning

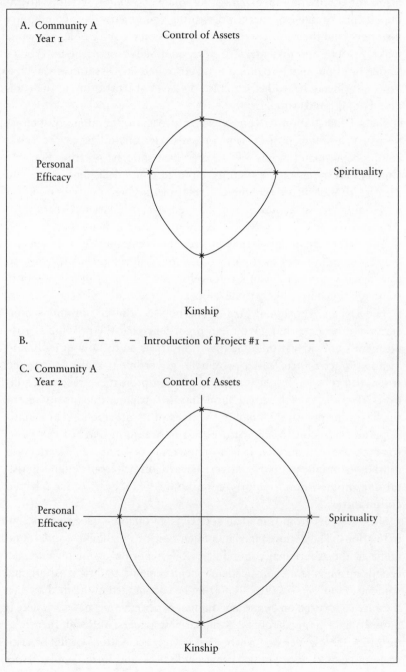

A. Community A
   Year 1   Control of Assets

Personal
Efficacy   Spirituality

                           Kinship

B.   – – – – – Introduction of Project #1 – – – – – –

C. Community A
   Year 2   Control of Assets

Personal
Efficacy   Spirituality

                           Kinship

are voiced in these communities. Can issues of contention be aired so that all sides can be examined in the name of solid decision-making?

Relationships between the selected communities and other communities and organizations may take the form of tribal councils or regional organizations based on treaty or national membership in Assembly of First Nations. Larger issues of policy are dealt with in these arenas, but regions and individual communities work effectively on specific issues linked to their immediate concerns.

Within these communities, there are examples of policies that support hiring on the basis of heritage and skills while consultants are used only in specific circumstances for limited time periods. This is not always possible when qualified applicants are unavailable, and so non-Aboriginal peoples carry those positions.

THE PLANNING TOOL

The Earth Mother enfolds the Elements of Development model. Figure 2 gives an example of using this model as a planning tool. Without the meaningful input of community discussion, this figure serves only as an example of one planning tool available to Aboriginal communities. Assuming the centre is o (weak) and the opposite end of each axis is 5, plot the number that best represents the community view of that particular axis. There are in fact sixteen axes, but for the purposes of illustration I use only the main four axes. After noting the number on each axes, connect the marks. This will show a pattern that can be used as a planning tool, in that the community can focus on aspects that are weak and select projects that will strengthen these essential elements of development. Often the goal is a circle of balanced elements.

This model can be used to evaluate the impact of potential projects on the community. Once a project is completed, community change can be documented. While financial information is critical to the success of projects, the evaluation need not stop there; qualitative information can be gathered about the impact on the community. FNDI uses this approach and includes such questions in the Measuring Change survey form:

Based on your experience, is this project:
• Based on tribe's traditional knowledge.
• Managed and facilitated by Natives.
• How much is the culture a part of the project?

What have you learned from this project? Have you learned:
• How to make healthier choices.
• Business skills.
• Social skills.
• Traditional skills.
• Something about your culture that you didn't know before.
• Parenting skills.
• About your own skills.
• Where your skills are needed in the community.
About other resources in the community:
• How has this project changed your life? ...
• How has your community changed? ...
• What would you change to make this project better?
• Tell us a story that shows what this project meant to you, your family or your community (FNDI, 1–2)

PARTNERSHIPS

Partnerships of all types are part of these communities' strategies for success. Tsuu T'ina Nation emphasizes the need for more band-owned enterprises, based on their lengthy experience. Their partnerships focus on specific expertise they value or on cultivating necessary relationships, as in the financial community. The Gwich'in have the resources to fund their own projects but will enter into advantageous partnerships. The partnerships that are examined in most detail in this study are the ones in which Bigstone Cree Nation has entered into agreements with resource companies. Two perspectives are examined: that of the community and the company.

Bigstone Cree Nation incorporates partnership opportunities into its economic development strategy. Bigstone's experiences are varied. It wants fairness in the opportunities that are made available to its members, recognition of its claim on its territory, and the spirit of the agreement observed as well as commitment to its terms. Bigstone acknowledges that training programs are costly and affect the bottom line, but it tries to work with companies in its area. The community must be assertive in setting the pace for significant partnerships through effective relationships.

Al Pac made its Aboriginal community policy integral to its corporate strategy. Clear feedback to that effect was one of the catalysts for a leading-edge industry policy. Al Pac reviewed community comments under the initial environmental-impact assessment process and sought advice from the Aboriginal community. As a result, the organization developed a number of internal and external programs. Internally, a senior manager acted as champion for this initiative, which saw it through start-up and lean times in the industry. Programs for understanding Aboriginal worldviews and ceremony were available for all staff. Supports were developed that encouraged retention of Aboriginal employees. A team was formed dedicated to the development and implementation of policies and programs both internally and externally. The point has been reached where knowledge and experience regarding Aboriginal issues are building throughout the organization.

Externally, community members hired by Al Pac made contact with various communities in the area. Initially they introduced senior Al Pac members to the leadership for discussions about company plans and the impact on the community. Relationships take time to cultivate, but in the end it makes good business sense from the perspectives of public relations, human resources, and operations. Al Pac wants a secure supply of raw material and so is committed to these policies.

Companies facing these decisions must come to terms with the reality that Aboriginal leadership and their communities are sophisticated business partners. Lip-service to these types of policies will be readily apparent and will sabotage long-term success. Al Pac is interested in the long term and as a result tries to balance supportive policies with crossing the line of business where it no longer makes sense. Is that enough, or should companies go further than what communities are demanding, going beyond the bottom line to what is right? Who determines what is right?

Mainstream companies make contracts available to Aboriginal-owned businesses but these Aboriginal companies are told that self-sufficiency is critical. Again, the mainstream company has to ask whether or not it has provided all that it can for these entrepreneurs. Communities' environmental concerns are generally acknowledged by mainstream businesses, but they must be part of the planning process that is put in place for community input so that meaningful plans are set. Taking the opportunity to share visions can influence policy and set the stage for successful partnerships.

Partnering is not an easy road. External obstacles may arise that are beyond the control of the company or community. As well, internal dissent regarding affirmative policies may sabotage these partnerships. Champions for the partnership with enough perseverance and authority to overcome the obstacles are needed in both camps. Both Al Pac and

Bigstone Cree Nation agree that their MOU has had mixed results. However, neither expressed intentions of giving up. Persistence is critical.

Sometimes time is the best tool. Over a period of years, Bigstone
members moved from a position of opposition to economic development to one of willingness to partner within pre-determined guidelines.
Within Al Pac, time and consistency of contact has encouraged an environment that integrates Aboriginal perspectives at many levels within
the company. This is not accomplished overnight.

Reviewing the relationship and continuing to build on it cannot be
taken for granted. People, priorities, and pressures change, and there
must be room to accommodate those changes. If problems arise, opportunities must be made for both sides to talk. For example, the Al
Pac/Bigstone MOU supports contracting opportunities, but it would ap-
pear that Al Pac thinks that offering the opportunity is enough, while
Bigstone wants more help in order to truly take advantage of the opportunity. Possible strategies might include dividing contracts into
manageable pieces for entrepreneurs or leasing expensive equipment to
entrepreneurs; this is an issue that must be negotiated. Here Al Pac has
an opportunity to make a decision that genuinely reflects concern and
caring for this community.

It is unclear how easily this model might be adapted in a setting where
a company had entrenched attitudes and procedures. Al Pac started business with commitment to working with Aboriginal peoples, although
this was new to many of its experienced forestry personnel. In any event,
there is much to be learned by the experience of Bigstone and Al Pac. Al
Pac's commitment has gone further than the company domain and ex-
tends to other companies in the industry. It is a priority to Al Pac's management that the forestry industry be a leader in promoting strong
relationships with Aboriginal communities. This commitment takes the
company policy to a different level and sets the company apart from
those who use meaningless employment statistics or set the bar of business opportunity in such a way that Aboriginal-owned companies cannot compete. An example of meaningless employment practice would be
to pump up part-time positions with Aboriginal peoples but then have
little or no reason for calling on part-time employees. Unfair business
practice might include a situation where expensive equipment is required
for bidding on contracts but the contracts are not large enough to support the cost of the equipment purchases.

Partnerships go beyond business, into community and government
relationships. For example, the Gwich'in form healthy alliances with

the non-members in their community and with other communities in the region. In Winnipeg the Aboriginal Council of Winnipeg (ACW) entered into a memorandum of understanding with municipal, provincial, and federal governments that supported its work and credibility with government. How committed these partners are to the well-being of urban-based Aboriginal peoples remains to be seen, especially in light of ACW's internal conflicts.

Economic development strategies taken by decision-makers in Aboriginal communities are based on the need to improve employment, training, and development initiatives in order to improve the quality of life enjoyed by their members. Community history, leadership, and connection to tradition affect the choice of appropriate and effective economic development approaches.

ABORIGINAL WISDOM

Wisdom encompasses the holistic view, possesses spiritual quality and is expressed in the experiential breadth and depth of life. (Newhouse, 1993, 95)

The connection to tradition has been labelled "Aboriginal wisdom." According to Ghostkeeper (personal communication, 1997), "wisdom" in economic development for Aboriginal peoples more aptly encompasses the ideas underlying the common western term of "sustainable development" – and goes beyond them. The knowledge caught and held in Aboriginal wisdom goes to the heart of sustainable development but then incorporates spirituality and ethics in ways that are not easily grasped by western practitioners. The holistic approach is the reason Aboriginal peoples survive, and that approach is encompassed in the concept of Aboriginal wisdom.

Aboriginal wisdom is not confined by age. Those communities that tap into the wisdom in all their members are guided in ways that best meet the needs of the community. Elders, youth, and women have roles with the men in their communities. They have a forum for their voices, including those that dissent. Strong communities are those that are most responsive to change, with leaders who are confident in hearing opinions and reaching decisions based on consensus. These roles are changing with the rhythms of modern times. There is still a place for wisdom, however, as demonstrated over and over in the communities studied in this book.

In their quest to understand life and the place of humankind, western scholars including Suzuki (1997), Daly (1994), Capra (1996), and

Hawken (1993) have picked up in their work the threads of Aboriginal wisdom. These approaches are manifested by the evolution of sustainable development to include policy, programs, and methodologies that share a connection with ancient Aboriginal wisdom that honours the gift of the Earth Mother. Most scholars do not often realize the extent of the connection nor do they dwell on it in their writing. It is indeed wondrous, however, to appreciate the greater wisdom that leads us on different paths to the same place.

Aboriginal wisdom is integral to the continued survival of Aboriginal peoples. It encompasses the cycles of life and death while seeking balance along the dimensions of being. It encompasses many of the goals of sustainable development as developed in the western world but draws together uniquely while going beyond the external rationale for honouring life's limitations. It is internalized for many but not all Aboriginal society members.

Aboriginal wisdom is discussed in the work of many Aboriginal scholars, among them Colorado (1988), Dockstater (1993), Newhouse (1992, 1993, 1997, 1998), Ghostkeeper (1993, 1996, 1997), Salway Black (1994), Alfred (1999), Simpson (1999), and Joe (2000). These thinkers ground their work in an acknowledgment of their heritage. It prods their philosophies. They offer perspectives on aspects of Aboriginal life that include economic development and have implications for Aboriginal communities, the business world, and policy setters.

That there is a place for Aboriginal wisdom is being recognized by more and more academic scholars (Addison Posey, 1999). What will the result be with the synthesis of these perspectives? Where will the impact be felt? Will it be allowed to influence the leaders of business and government to bring us to a different place than the one we are currently headed for? A chorus of approaches is coming from many different disciplines and is synchronized around the same song: a common understanding of the need for meaningful change.

ABORIGINAL WISDOM IN PRACTICE: CONCLUSIONS

Aboriginal peoples declare again and again that "the land is our life, our home, and must be protected." It is a given that sets the stage for many Aboriginal leaders to make decisions that respect the land as well as meet their community demands for employment opportunities. The land is a resource to be used by communities to look after themselves in independence. This may result in a superficial assessment by outsiders labelling certain decisions as the antithesis of sustainable development principles (Widdowson & Howard, 1998). Sometimes understanding and deeper appreciation may result after examining the community's decision in these situations. In other cases, Aboriginal communities may maximize resource use as unsustainably as those in the mainstream economy.

For many Aboriginal people, the connection to the land is so integral to their personal identities that it is a surprise to even be asked to talk about it. This does not mean that all Aboriginal peoples have an innate attachment to Mother Earth or that each will act on it when given the chance. It does means that when Aboriginal communities are able to make consistent input into the decision-making process, the checks and balances in the system will tend to factor protection of the Earth Mother into the final decision.

For example, Tsuu T'ina Nation decided against a profitable business proposal for its business park because the by-products from the service work would be harmful to the environment. Tsuu T'ina Nation businesses must be passed by the elders council, chief and council, and community and meet the Nation's zoning by-law that fully addresses environmental issues.

Bigstone Cree Nation has taken a very cautious approach to the economic development of resources. Though initially not interested in the forestry industry, ten years later they were more open to partnerships but still cautious and concerned to protect their resources. This community is interested in partnerships and business opportunities that will still allow them to satisfy community standards regarding the environment. They are aggressive in protecting their land, and when new companies come to exploit resources without proper consultation, the Nation acts quickly to defend their children's heritage. The province may have awarded proper licences, but the norm in the community is now that companies are being required to act responsibly.

The Gwich'in people are most articulate about their continuing ties to the land, celebrating those families who spend time on the land during weekends or holidays. This is an important factor in their investment decisions because they want to preserve the land for future generations, also noted by their elders. None of these communities has demonstrated priorities where profit is given precedence hand in hand with destruction of land. Rather, the guiding principle is reasonable development in support of livelihood and community.

However, individual interests are more prominent in the urban setting, where community is made up of organizations that attract individuals with common interests – a construct of a multitude of communities. In terms of sustainability, this setting requires a shift of focus from natural resources to institutional sustainability through leadership foresight, human resource development, and financial resource allocation. The Aboriginal Centre remains a nucleus for the Aboriginal community as it houses a number of businesses and organizations within the larger Neeginan project. It is profitable and represents a major real-estate investment held by members of the Aboriginal community. Debate continues about the sustainability of this centralizing approach compared to investing in a number of less risky projects in keeping with the needs of the community. Further, reliance on government funding that finance budgets of tenants puts the centre in a position of risk for the long term.

The Aboriginal Council of Winnipeg (ACW) provides an alternative to the Manitoba Métis Fédération (MMF) and the Assembly of Manitoba Chiefs (AMC) who, due to resource constraints, have not moved quickly to meet the needs of their urban-based members. As this changes, ACW's strengths lie in the vision for an independent organization that does not provide services but nurtures the ones that need help. Its leadership must regain balance and move forward in gaining greater membership and encouraging participation in decisions. ACW's mandate makes the organization available to all Aboriginal peoples in the city of Winnipeg, going beyond the membership-based mandates of MMF and AMC. Its inclusive approach contributes to its sustainability. Where priority is instead given to maintenance of the status quo rather than support for young leaders with new visions, this works against the continuing health of Aboriginal organizations and communities.

Community rhythms allude to the main axes in the Elements of Development model, including control of assets, spirituality, kinship, and personal efficacy as well as to the internal/external challenges and opportunities facing each community. Each community must walk its own path and live its own truth. Each has similar problems that are shaped by local circumstances that make them distinctive. Although they can learn from each other's experience, they will have to reach further for the significance which that experience has for their community rather than just try to "rubber-stamp" experiences from one community to another.

Corporate Canada shows a willingness to work with Aboriginal communities when it makes good business sense. Different standards to reflect Aboriginal employee differences do not work unless company policies are revised in a manner that makes sense for everyone. The usual starting point in considering these questions is the business orientation to the bottom line. Generally, Aboriginal peoples are expected to fit into the corporate culture. Room for kinship, spirituality, and personal efficacy are not priorities, since they do not translate directly into profits. Is there room in the business world for Aboriginal perspectives and priorities? Is there a way that time pressures may be eased to let the cycles of nature dictate pace, focus, and balance? What differences would a more holistic approach make in the boardrooms of corporate Canada? I submit that it is time to find out.

Aboriginal companies and organizations are able to give more room to these rhythms when business is being done in their own communities where Nation members have control. In the mainstream business world, traditions such as ceremonies or honouring the collective nature of Aboriginal communities oftentimes are seen as burdensome or meaningless. Acknowledging that the single-minded focus on profit as the norm, to the exclusion of balance and respect, has significantly marred the quality of life for future generations is a giant step towards realizing that capitalism in its present form does not have all the answers. It is time once again for Aboriginal peoples to share survival skills with their brothers and sisters for the benefit of this generation and all those that follow.

Profit is important, but it is not the only factor to consider in a business decision. For example, truly effective partnerships go past lip service to commitment at senior levels to creative programs and policies that actually make a difference and go even beyond the demands of Aboriginal communities. Time must be given for relationships to develop and for progress to be made. This includes building an internal climate that supports these policies.

The communities in this study demonstrate the level of activity occurring across the country. I have highlighted community members who are proactive, insightful, and visionary. When they have the skills and control, they focus on the community vision in ways that cannot be dictated nor handed to them by outsiders. Governing is not easy, but individuals with reasons to dedicate their time to the process are stepping forward to listen and be guided in traditions that are appropriate to their communities. They approach economic development on their terms. Many are assuming control of programming in all areas at a pace that flies in the face of the picture of dependence commonly understood by Canadians.

In the effective governance of business projects, these communities have dealt with the issue of separating business and politics in their own ways. It is not an either/or situation as is painted by some research studies (RCAP, vol. 2, 1996). For example, Bigstone Cree Nation says that at this stage in its development, it is satisfied with chief and council being involved in business decisions including investment and policy issues. This saves time since there is always a political element that must be dealt with. The arrangement may change as the community grows, but for now it works. On the other hand, Tsuu T'ina has recognized the political element but also the need for input from community members with business expertise. They structure their board membership with a majority of community members but with participation by a band councillor. Thus politics does not overwhelm the process but maintains a presence.

Finding the appropriate balance is always challenging. The Aboriginal Business Development Centre went through a change in management that, according to their funders, was related to an ineffective mixing of political and business agendas. The issue at hand is that for Aboriginal peoples the time to learn all types of lessons is now. A guiding hand is useful, but sometimes hard lessons are the best.

The time is past for maintaining separation of services because of the political labels placed on Aboriginal peoples by colonizing forces. The approach taken by the Aboriginal Centre, the Aboriginal Council of Winnipeg, and other organizations meeting the needs of Aboriginal peoples is much more satisfying and in keeping with Aboriginal traditions. Although government funding may be an excuse to continue former practices, more meaningful self-governance and independence is demonstrated by new partnerships of sharing and caring that honour our traditions, moving in directions where Aboriginal peoples recognize common needs and work together to make new realities.

Daly, Suzuki, Hawken, and Capra, thinkers who are exploring the boundaries of conventional theory in their diverse disciplines, point to the role of Aboriginal wisdom in economic development. Other writers such as Berkes, Elias, Wien, and Loxley conduct research with Aboriginal peoples regarding economic development choices in ways that respectfully acknowledge opportunities, strengths, and challenges. For Aboriginal scholars such as Salway Black, Newhouse, Dockstater, Ghostkeeper, and Colorado, the wisdom that flows from their worldviews directs their research, which includes economic development in their communities. The First Nations Development Institute uses community wisdom as a guide in encouraging development. Aboriginal worldviews warrant more attention in economic development literature, with the stage set for Aboriginal scholars to carry their wisdom forward in exploration of economic development for Aboriginal society.

Aboriginal communities will continue to draw on wisdom from mainstream business as well as their own experience and perspectives in developing strategies for economic development. Without some period of reflection, capitalism could easily be followed without thought of consequences. These blended approaches may flourish in the future especially with support from those who understand the importance of Aboriginal wisdom in the process.

This scrutiny of selected Aboriginal communities demonstrates evidence of a rich heritage that is cherished even in an urban setting. Aboriginal wisdom has a presence that is stronger in some communities than in others, but its role is evident in all their community economic development strategies. To expect systematic application of Aboriginal wisdom even within Aboriginal society is unrealistic and would not respect the diversity inherent in Aboriginal communities; yet its contribution to the continued survival of Aboriginal peoples cannot be underestimated.

Many challenges lie ahead for these communities on their particular journeys to independence. It is crucial for Aboriginal peoples to be able to contribute to Canadian society in positive ways, since the more common experience is negative. Acknowledging and using Aboriginal experience and insight where it can benefit both Aboriginal communities and Canadian society is a win-win situation. The stories of the struggles and triumphs of individual Aboriginal communities can serve as evaluative guides for policy, appropriate economic development strategies, and insight into specific approaches to questions of resources, human development, and other governance issues.

Further participatory research in these areas will increase understanding of what works and how assistance can be most thoughtfully employed to help those striving for strong communities. Such research must continue to draw on the strengths of Aboriginal wisdom and ways of knowing in partnership with western approaches. When we talk generally about what should be done or what is being done, the message goes just so far. It is apparent to those who are close to these communities and their experiences, of course, but it usually is deflected by walls of indifference and ignorance that separate Aboriginal peoples from the rest of Canadians. A clearer picture emerges when the message is told in the words of community members. That is the best of what comes from sharing and caring.

Self-reflection is one of many ways Aboriginal peoples traditionally learned how to live a good life, since lessons for survival were gathered and passed on in families and communities. The act of contemplation is common to many people in this world who halt the busyness of modern living to savour moments and give thanks to a greater force, be that God, Creator, the Love of Life, or something else. This project has strengthened my conviction that spirit has been ignored or segregated in a western approach from most things including economic development decisions and that this has been at great cost.

I give thanks for the opportunity to know the people I interviewed for a little while and to be filled with such energy for the possibilities in our communities. It is people who bring government development theories or business strategy to life, and I am honoured to share my knowledge of the people in our communities who are making a difference. As a modern Aboriginal scholar and a woman, I am very interested in the role of women in economic development. I wanted to know where young people and community elders fit in the process, to know what thought is given to the Earth Mother. I wanted to know whether we bring our own perspective to economic development. I was enlightened by the results of this project.

I opened the door on the lives of these people and then closed it, only to honour you now by standing aside and letting you explore these paths for yourself. The preceding thoughts express my journey, as I can only speak of what I know; but I am convinced that Aboriginal perspectives are essential to the survival of the Earth Mother and our communities.

The changes continue in these communities and are heartening. Sharing stories, dreams, and victories makes us all strong, in tune with our living rhythms.

I also invite each of you to extend your hand in friendship to a community, company, or organization profiled in this book. You may say thanks or you may want to talk about experiences. I guarantee that it will be an investment with an enormous return.

Here are their addresses:

Aboriginal Centre Administrative Office
181 Higgins Ave.
Winnipeg, MB
R3B 3G1

Aboriginal Council of Winnipeg
181 Higgins Ave.
Winnipeg, MB
R3B 3GI

Alberta Pacific Forest Industries, Inc.
PO Box 8000
Boyle, AB
TOA OMO

Bigstone Cree Nation
PO Box 960
Desmarais, AB
TOG OTO

Gwich'in Band Office
Fort McPherson, NT
XOE OJO

St Theresa Point First Nation
General Delivery
St Theresa Point, MB
ROB IJO

The North West Company
77 Main Street
Winnipeg, MB
R3C 2RI

Tla-o-qui-aht First Nation
PO Box 18
Tofino, BC
VOR 2ZO

Toquaht First Nation
PO Box 759
Ucluelet, BC
VOR 2ZO

Tsuu T'ina Nation
Administration Building
9911 Chula Blvd
Tsuu T'ina, AB
T2W 6H6

Tribal Councils Investment Group
2190–360 Main Street
Winnipeg, MB
R3C 3Z3

References

Addison Posey, Darrell. 1999. *Cultural and spiritual values of biodiversity.* London: Intermediate Technology Publications.

Alfred, T. 1999. *Peace, power, righteousness: An indigenous manifesto.* Don Mills, Ont.: Oxford University Press.

Berkes, F. 1999. *Sacred ecology: Traditional ecological knowledge and resource management.* Philadelphia: Taylor & Francis.

Capra, F. 1996. *The web of life: A new scientific understanding of living systems.* New York: Anchor Books.

Cash, M. 2000. Best customers are owners now: Aboriginal consortium buys piece of North West Company. *Winnipeg Free Press,* 15 July, B1.

Colorado, P. 1988. Bridging native and western science. *Convergence* 21, 49–67.

Daly, H., and J. Cobb. 1994. *For the common good: Redirecting the economy toward community, the environment, and a sustainable future.* Boston: Beacon Press.

Dockstater, Mark. 1993. Towards an understanding of Aboriginal self-government: A proposed theoretical model and illustrative factual analysis. Ph.D. diss., Osgoode Hall Law School, York University, North York, Ont.

Elias, P. 1997. *Development of Aboriginal peoples' communities.* North York, Ont.: Centre for Aboriginal Management Education and Training/Captus Press.

– 1995. *Northern Aboriginal communities: Economies and development.* North York, Ont.: Captus Press.

First Nations Development Institute. 1996–97. *Annual report.* Fredericksburg, Va.: FNDI.

– 1997. *Biennial report, 1996–97.* Fredericksburg, Va.

– n.d. Measuring change. Survey form. Fredericksburg, Va.

Ghostkeeper, E. 1993. Spiritual economics. Paper presented at a conference of the Yukon Community Futures Committee, Whitehorse, Yukon.

- 1996. *Spirit gifting: The concept of spiritual exchange.* Calgary: The Arctic Institute of North America.
- 1997. Telephone interview by author with Métis scholar and elder, residing in Spruce Grove, Alta., 4 November.

Gwich'in Financial Road Map. 1994. Developed by delegates at the Gwich'in Financial Roundtable, Whitehorse, Yukon. Arctic Institute of North America: University of Calgary.

Hawken, P. 1993. *The ecology of commerce: A declaration of sustainability.* New York: HarperCollins.

Henderson, H. 1978. *Creating alternative futures.* New York: Berkley.

Indian and Northern Affaires, Tsuu T'ina Nation. Community Profiles Online: <http://sdiprod2.inac.gc.ca/FNProfiles/FNProfiles>

Joe, J. 2000. Behind the curtain of words: Diabetic complications and re-definition of self. In *Aboriginal Health, Identity and Resources,* edited by J. Oakes, R. Riewe, S. Koolage, L. Simpson, and N. Schuster. Winnipeg: University of Manitoba, 8–21.

Lendsay, K., and W. Wuttunee. 1997. Historical economic perspectives of Aboriginal peoples: Cycles of balance and partnership. In *Cost of doing nothing: A call to action.* CANDO/Royal Bank of Canada Symposium. Toronto: Royal Bank of Canada. (Available from the Royal Bank of Canada, Royal Bank Plaza, Toronto, ON, M5J 2J5).

Loxley, J. 1992. Manitoba: The dynamics of north-south relationships. In *People and land in Northern Manitoba,* edited by Y. Lithman, R. Riewe, R. Wiest, and L. Wrigley. University of Manitoba Anthropology Papers No. 32, 55–64.
- 2000. Aboriginal economic development in Winnipeg. Unpublished manuscript, University of Manitoba.

Masuzumi, B. 1998. Presentation to university course no. 2:420, First Nations Government, University of Manitoba, by special advisor on traditional knowledge to the Government of the Northwest Territories.

McCann, P., Fullgrabe, K., and Godfrey-Smith, W. 1984. *Social implications of technological change.* Canberra: Department of Science and Technology.

Neel, D. 1992. *Our chiefs and elders: Words and photographs of native leaders.* Vancouver: UBC Press.

Newhouse, D. 1992. From the tribal to the modern: The development of modern Aboriginal societies. Unpublished submission to the Royal Commission on Aboriginal Peoples. Native Studies, Trent University, Peterborough, Ont.
- 1993. Modern Aboriginal economies: Capitalism with an Aboriginal face. In *Sharing the Harvest: The Road to Self-Reliance.* National Roundtable on Aboriginal Economic Development and Resources, 90–100. Ottawa: Royal Commission on Aboriginal Peoples.

– 1998. Resistance is futile: Aboriginal peoples meet the borg of capitalism. Paper presented at the Bank of Montreal Distinguished Visitor Speakers Series, 8 February 1998.

Newhouse, D., and C. Mount-Pleasant Jetté. 1997. CANDO statement on the economic development recommendations of the Royal Commission on Aboriginal peoples. In *The cost of doing nothing: A call to action*. The Joint CANDO-Royal Bank Symposium, Toronto, Ontario. (Available from the Royal Bank of Canada, Royal Bank Plaza, Toronto, ON, M5J 2J5).

Nuu-Chah-Nulth Tribal Council. 1998. The Nuu-Chah-Nulth tribal council. http://www.nuuchahnulth.org/index.html. 21 April 2000.

Polyani, K. 1957. *The great transformation*. 1944. Reprint, Boston: Beacon.

Rosborough, L. 1997. Suzuki can't save the earth by himself. *Winnipeg Free Press*, 4 November, D6.

Royal Commission on Aboriginal Peoples. 1996. *Looking forward, looking back*. Ottawa: Canada Communication Group.

– 1996a. Vol. 2: *Restructuring the relationship*. Part 1 and part 2. Ottawa: Canada Communication Group.

– 1996b. Vol. 3: *Gathering strength*. Ottawa: Canada Communication Group.

– 1996c. Vol. 4: *Perspectives and realities*. Ottawa: Canada Communication Group.

Salway Black, S. 1994. Redefining success in community development: A new approach for determining and measuring the impact of development. The 1994 Richard Shramm Paper on Community Development. Presented at the Lincoln Filene Centre.

Schumpeter, J. 1975. The future of private enterprise in the face of modern socialistic tendencies. *History of Political Economy* 7, no.3, 294–298.

Scientific Panel for Sustainable Forest Practices in Clayoquot Sound. 1995. *First Nations perspectives relating to forest practices standards in Clayoquot Sound*. Victoria, B.C.: Crown Publications.

Simpson, L. 1999. The construction of traditional ecological knowledge: Issues, implications and insights. Ph.D. diss., University of Manitoba, Winnipeg.

– 2000. Anishinaabe ways of knowing. In *Aboriginal health, identity and resources*, edited by J. Oakes, R. Riewe, S. Koolage, L. Simpson, and N. Schuster. Winnipeg: University of Manitoba.

Society of Management Accountants of Canada. 1996. Accounting for sustainable development: A business perspective. *Management Accounting Issues* Paper 14.

Suzuki, D., and A. McConnell. 1997. *The sacred balance: Rediscovering our place in nature*. Vancouver: Douglas & McIntyre.

Tribal Councils Investment Group of Manitoba Ltd. 1997. Unpublished report. Winnipeg.

Ward, S. 1997. Collaborative research in Nunavut: The case of the Mallik Island Park study, Cape Dorset, NWT. Master's thesis, Natural Resources Institute, University of Manitoba, Winnipeg.

Weiskopf, W. 1971. *Alienation and economics*. New York: Dutton.

Index